Contents

The Week That Changed the World

The Message That Changes Lives

The
Agony & Glory
of the Cross

A gift from the:

Valley Church of Christ

29035 Del Monte Drive

Sun City, CA 92586

www.valleycofcsc.org

Ph # (951) 679-1010

The Agony & Glory of the Cross

Charles B. Hodge, Jr.

Truth for Today
World Mission School
P.O. Box 2044
Searcy, AR 72145-2044

ISBN-13: 978-0-9795390-6-0
ISBN-10: 0-9795390-6-4

A Note to the Reader

The heart of the New Testament is the crucifixion of Jesus. Therefore, this study of His death will bring you to the subject that is above all other subjects that God wants you to hear, meditate upon, and understand. Nothing in your life is more important than understanding what Jesus did for you and responding to His great gift in the way the New Testament describes. This book invites you to study carefully the New Testament and grasp the divine sacrifice that was made for you, and through your obedience to its message, take your stand at the foot of His cross. Your true happiness in this life, and your eternal salvation in the life to come, rest upon your relationship to His cross. Remember, "the word of the cross is foolishness to those who are perishing, but to us who are being saved it is the power of God" (1 Corinthians 1:18).

The last page of this book has e-mail addresses and postal addresses where you can write to receive additional encouragement as you seek to walk with Jesus into eternal life. A companion book, *Into the Abundant Life*, details the way one can live the abundant life that Jesus has provided for us. That book contains a New Testament to help you continue your study of God's Word. Send us a note and let us know that you want it, and we will make sure you get it.

A Note from the Author

The Bible has only one message . . . the cross. Paul said, "For I determined to know nothing among you except Jesus Christ, and Him crucified" (1 Corinthians 2:2). We love God's Word and quote it, yet we must give greater diligence to studying it and living it. While we wear the cross as jewelry and use it on our signs, it was meant to be worn on the heart.

The cross brought the death of Jesus. It was gory, bloody, and heart-wrenching. While writing is difficult for me, writing about the cross is more difficult. When human hands touch the cross, they defile it. No one can do justice to it by writing a book about it. This study of the cross has grown out of a wrestling match within me. As I wrote it, I knew that I was standing on holy ground and would not be able to express the depth of the biblical teaching. It has been humbling, overwhelming, and yet rewarding. The cross is not superficial—it is the depth of all knowledge! Every human being must come to "know" the Christ and His cross! It is the glory of all who are saved.

We must not try to embellish the cross. It needs no commentary. As you study these lessons, allow the cross to speak for itself. Let the Scriptures lead you to the foot of the cross, where salvation is found.

"God forbid that I should glory,
save in the cross of our Lord Jesus Christ"
(Galatians 6:14a; KJV).

Charles B. Hodge, Jr.

1

Sunday

Matthew 21:1–11; 26:6–13;
Mark 11:1–11; 14:3–9; Luke 19:29–44;
John 12:1–19

"As He was going, they were spreading their coats on the road. As soon as He was approaching, near the descent of the Mount of Olives, the whole crowd of the disciples began to praise God joyfully with a loud voice . . ." (Luke 19:36, 37).

What a day! What a week! This was the beginning of the week when God's Son, Jesus, died! It was the week of God's greatest work—His work through the cross! It was the week that changed the world and the week that changed me!

When the details are put together, the Bible reveals only forty-plus days in the life of Christ, yet the divine narration of the week of His death gives numerous details concerning His activities. What Jesus did in this one week consumes one-third of the New Testament books of Matthew, Mark, Luke, and John; it makes up one-half of the Gospel of John. The mere space given to it tells us that this week is all-important.

During His ministry, Jesus did not spend much time in Jerusalem. Now, He set His face to go to Jerusalem

1

(Luke 9:51). He was in total control; He went to Jerusalem to die.

What did Jesus do during this time? He taught! He was teaching even on the cross! The Jews claimed that they wanted the Messiah[1]; yet, when He came, they had Him crucified! He did not fulfill their concept of a Messiah. Does He fit ours? Can we accept the biblical Christ?

Let us look at the Sunday of the week that changed the world. All eternity depends on what Jesus did in this week and how we respond to it.

THE ANOINTING

The first event on Sunday was the anointing of Jesus (Matthew 26:6–13; Mark 14:3–9; John 12:1–8). He was at Bethany in the house of Simon the leper: "So they made Him a supper there, and Martha was serving; but Lazarus was one of those reclining at the table with Him" (John 12:2).[2] At the supper, Mary anointed Jesus with expensive oil. Its worth was approximately a year's wages for a common man.

We see here the lesson of receiving. Throughout His life Jesus had given. Perhaps it is easier to give than to receive in times of crisis, but Jesus taught both.

The true character of Judas surfaces here as he said, "Why was this perfume not sold for three hundred denarii and given to poor people? . . ." (John 12:4–6). It is amazing

---

[1]"Messiah," from a Hebrew word meaning "anointed," is the equivalent of the Greek word "Christ" (see John 1:41; 4:25).

[2]This event was on Saturday evening according to our time. While our day begins at 12 midnight, the Jewish day began at 6 p.m. Therefore, this supper took place as Sunday began. John gave chronological clues regarding the event: (1) Jesus arrived in the town of Bethany six days before the Passover (John 12:1), and (2) His Triumphal Entry took place "on the next day" after the meal (John 12:12).

how the apostles[3] thought they could openly criticize Jesus! Their rebuke of Jesus was harsh and disrespectful.

Benevolence is a blessing to us and to others, but serving Jesus is of even greater importance than benevolence. Whatever is given to Jesus *for* Jesus cannot be thought of as "waste." Jesus exposed Judas' guilty motives, and He honored Mary's extravagant gift of love. Anything love gives to Jesus is always too little.

Another lesson we see in this setting is that true friends are costly. Earlier Jesus had raised His friend Lazarus from the dead (John 11). That resurrection became part of the Jews' motivation to crucify Jesus. Our good works can sometimes cause hate and persecution.

THE TRIUMPHAL ENTRY

Jesus had never had a "praise welcome." He chose to have one here (see Matthew 21:1–11; Mark 11:1–11; Luke 19:29–44; John 12:12–15). He got on a donkey and rode into town as the King of the Jews. In doing so, He forced people to make a decision about Him. "Accept Me or kill Me!" He was saying. He carefully planned His "Triumphal Entry."

He sent two disciples[4] to get a colt that had never been ridden. This is amazing! The colt's owner must have known and believed in Jesus. Jesus had to borrow a donkey because He was a "Penniless King." He went to the subjects; usually subjects go to their king.

The people spread branches and clothes upon the

---

[3]The apostles were "sent-out" messengers. They were the twelve men chosen by Jesus to help spread His kingdom (see Luke 6:13–16).

[4]"Disciples" means "followers" or "learners." This word is sometimes used generally for followers of Jesus (see Matthew 9:14) and sometimes specifically for the twelve apostles (see Matthew 10:1).

3

road before Him. They shouted, "Hosanna," which means "Save, we pray." His jubilant entrance fulfilled the prophecy found in Zechariah 9:9.

As Jesus arrived at Jerusalem, He was overcome with emotion—His heart broke with sorrow. He cried over Jerusalem (Luke 19:41). He wept audibly over those who were going to reject Him. Jerusalem had been God's chosen city. Ten thousand memories were vanishing; time was running out. Jerusalem was about to be totally destroyed (A.D. 67–70).

Jesus rode peacefully into town on the donkey. His actions did not bother the Romans who would soon be crucifying Him.

The crowd on Sunday was made up of Galileans; but the one on Thursday and Friday was Judean, and that crowd cried for His death. When the Prince of Peace came to town, He was honored with songs of praise. However, this forced His enemies to take action. They thought the world was following Him (John 12:19).

The Pharisees were horrified! They commanded Jesus to rebuke (or silence) His disciples, but Jesus refused. If His disciples had not praised Him, the stones would have cried out with praise of Him (Luke 19:40). This "praise welcome" was monumental. While Jerusalem had refused to *listen*, the people could not fail to *see*!

Jesus had His "praise welcome." Will we give Him one?

The cross . . .
there is no other way!

2

Monday

Matthew 21:12–17; Mark 11:12–19;
Luke 19:45–48; John 12:20–50

*"And Jesus entered the temple and drove out all those who
were buying and selling. . . . And the blind and the lame came to
Him in the temple, and He healed them" (Matthew 21:12–14).*

Jesus had now arrived in Jerusalem. He would never
be "Man of the Year" on the cover of a magazine or receive
the Nobel Peace Prize, but He became our Savior! He rode
on a donkey (a symbol of peace), He did not ride on a
horse (a symbol of war). Since Solomon, no king had ridden into town on a donkey (see 1 Kings 1:38).

The issue, as always, was authority. On this day,
Monday, Jesus would present His credentials.

JESUS CURSED A FIG TREE

Jesus was hungry. He saw a fig tree with leaves and
was disappointed to find no fruit. He condemned this
tree forever (see Matthew 21:18–22; Mark 11:12–14, 20–26).
This is not the Jesus most of us have created in our minds.
His action on this occasion is one of only two negative
(destructive) miracles that Jesus performed during His
ministry (see Matthew 8:28–34). It harmed nature, but not

humanity. He was giving an object lesson that the apostles had to learn. The sin was pride and hypocrisy. The fig tree claimed to have fruit. It did not. Jewish leaders claimed to be of God. They were not. The Jews should have been humbled to be called by God. Instead, they thought they were superior and invincible.

Peter was amazed by the sudden death of that fig tree. Why? The apostles had seen Jesus walk on water, heal the sick, and raise the dead. Still, they were shocked to see the fig tree wither at Jesus' command!

JESUS CLEANSED THE TEMPLE

Next, Jesus went to the temple. Without introduction, He began teaching. On the side, He healed the blind and the lame (see Matthew 21:12–16; Mark 11:15–18; Luke 19:45–48). The chief priests and the scribes saw the marvelous things He did (Matthew 21:15) and were surely made aware of His deity.

The temple area was to be reverenced, but it was being abused! The people were using it as a shortcut through Jerusalem; they were using it as a place to exercise avarice and greed.

The Jews had to pay the temple tax with the Hebrew shekel. Those coming to Jerusalem had to exchange their Roman denarii or Greek drachmas for temple shekels in order to pay the tax. The money changers charged an exorbitant amount to exchange the worshipers' money.

As He cleansed the temple, Jesus did not attack men, but He did chase them away. He did rearrange the furniture. He quoted the Bible: "'My house shall be called a house of prayer'; but you are making it a robbers' den" (Matthew 21:13; see Jeremiah 7:11). He was not a coward or a "sissy." He was a "man among men." He not only was physically strong, but He also used the Scriptures mightily. His language was pointed and true.

JESUS CONTINUED HIS TEACHING

In the midst of all this, a delegation of Greeks came, wanting to see Jesus (John 12:20-50).[1] While the Jews sought to kill Him, the Greeks sought to hear Him! Philip was always bringing someone to Jesus. He partnered up with Andrew, and they approached Jesus. Jesus knew "His hour" had come, yet He continued to teach profound truths. He taught that seed must die to live and that those who love their lives will lose them (John 12:21–26).

Then Jesus said in the presence of others who had gathered, "Father, glorify Your name." For the third time during His life, a voice spoke out of heaven (John 12:28). To some it sounded like thunder, but to Jesus it was a promise of victory. Satan was to be cast out by His death. Jesus declared at this time, "And I, if I am lifted up from the earth, will draw all men to Myself" (John 12:32).

In spite of this glorious teaching that was accompanied by a mighty miracle, the religious leaders refused to believe. John concluded, ". . . they loved the approval of men rather than the approval of God" (John 12:42, 43).

The cross . . .
there is no other way!

---

[1]Commentators are not agreed as to whether this discourse was given on Monday or Tuesday. It is the only incident found in the Gospel of John between the Triumphal Entry on Sunday and the Last Supper on Friday.

3

Tuesday

Matthew 21:18—25:46; Mark 11:20—13:37;
Luke 20; 21; John 12:20-50

*"Then they sent some of the Pharisees and Herodians to
Him in order to trap Him in a statement" (Mark 12:13).*

Of all the days recorded in the Scriptures, Tuesday
was the busiest day in the life of Christ. When He had
cleansed the temple, He hit the Jewish leaders in their
pocketbooks. This got their attention. The Jewish leaders
had made a "robbers' den" out of the temple.

They became angry with Jesus and asked, "Where
did You get Your authority?"; "Who are You?"; "Who do
You think You are?" They thought they could quickly run
this Galilean out of town. If He answered them by saying,
"God," He lost, for they would charge Him with blasphemy. If He answered them by saying, "Man," He still
lost, for they would say He had no right to do what He
had done. However, Jesus turned the situation around by
asking, "Where did John get his authority?" Jesus fought
fire with fire. They refused to answer Him, so Jesus did
not answer them! (See Matthew 21:23–27; Mark 11:27–33;
Luke 20:1–8.) The Jewish leaders tried to demean Jesus by
asking for His credentials: "Where did You go to school?

You are not a priest, an ordained rabbi, or a graduate of Jerusalem Seminary." They soon found out that He was "The Great Debater." He exposed their foolishness.

LESSONS IN PARABLES

Jesus taught three parables in this context. The apostles asked Jesus why He taught in parables and what He meant (Matthew 13:10, 36). He said that this practice eliminated those who were merely curious from being among His followers. Parables are not "children's stories." They gently guide you into convicting yourself.

Jesus first presented a parable of two sons, illustrating what repentance is (Matthew 21:28–32). One son refused to obey his father and then repented and obeyed, while the other told his father he would obey but later did not. Publicans (or tax collectors) and harlots will enter into God's presence when some "religious folk" will not. Publicans and harlots did not crucify Jesus. This was done by God's nation, Israel. Jerusalem was God's city. Inside Jerusalem was God's temple, but just outside the city walls Jesus would soon be crucified. It is shocking to see how vicious, blind, proud, and prejudiced religionists can be.

Next, Jesus told a parable of wicked renters who killed the landlord's son, illustrating how He would be rejected (Matthew 21:33–44; Mark 12:1–12; Luke 20:9–19). He spoke of the stone that could have saved Israel but was cast aside. The Jewish leaders knew that Jesus was talking about them and Himself.

He told a parable of a marriage feast, showing how some would reject His invitation (Matthew 22:2–14; Luke 14:16–24). Relatives and friends not only rejected the invitation, but they even used the occasion for murderous sport. The king who was having the wedding for his son was furious and said, "Go therefore to the main highways, and as many as you find there, invite to the wedding feast" (Matthew 22:9). When the privileged shut themselves out, the common were invited. No wonder the common people heard Jesus gladly (Mark 12:37).

DEBATES BEGIN

Soon the Pharisees and the Herodians[1] came together to entangle Jesus in His words. The Pharisees hated the Herodians and believed they were traitors—but they hated Jesus more. The two groups presented a trick question to Jesus: "What about the poll tax?" Jesus, holding a coin, said, "Render to Caesar the things that are Caesar's; and to God the things that are God's" (Matthew 22:21). This shocked them into silence.

When the Sadducees[2] came to Him, they only offered silliness. Jesus was direct with them. He said, "You don't know the Scriptures" and "You don't know the power of God" (Matthew 22:29; Mark 12:24).

The persistent Pharisees returned with a lawyer, who asked, "What is the greatest command?" Jesus answered, "Love God foremost," and then added the second greatest command: "Love your neighbor as yourself." His answer silenced the lawyer. (See Matthew 22:34–40; Mark 12:28–34.)

Jesus then asked them who the Messiah really was. They gave no response. At this point, the debates ended. (See Matthew 22:41–46; Mark 12:35–37; Luke 20:41–44.)

---

[1]Perhaps the most influential Jewish religious leaders in Jesus' day, the Pharisees were characterized as self-righteous and legalistic. The Herodians were a political group dedicated to increasing the power of Herod's family in Palestine.

[2]The Sadducees were wealthy aristrocrats, many of whom were priests. They hated Jesus because He threatened their authority.

A POINTED SERMON

Following all of this, Jesus preached the most scathing sermon in the Scriptures (Matthew 23). He called the Jewish leaders "snakes" and "blind guides." He pronounced seven woes, branding them "hypocrites." "How can you escape the condemnation of hell?" He asked them. Then He cried, "Jerusalem, Jerusalem . . . ! How often I wanted to gather your children together, . . . and you were unwilling" (Matthew 23:37; see Luke 13:34).

PROPHECY AND PREACHING

As they walked away from the temple, His disciples asked Jesus three questions about the fall of the temple: "When will these things be?"; "What will be the sign of Your coming?"; "When is the end of the age?" Jesus dealt with these questions in Matthew 24, Mark 13, and Luke 21. In other words, He was still teaching.

Here we read of "the widow with the two mites" who gave all she had to God (Mark 12:41–44; Luke 21:1–4). Amidst all the hypocrisy, God sent this humble widow to remind all people for all time what true giving to God actually is! What a God!

Trouble was ahead! In spite of the crowds and the critics, Jesus taught His disciples three more profound parables: a parable of ten virgins, emphasizing preparedness; a parable of talents, stressing responsibility; and a parable of sheep and goats, picturing the judgment (Matthew 25). No servant of God ever preached as Jesus did that day, but His preaching fell on deaf ears.

What a day!

The cross . . .
there is no other way!

11

4
Wednesday, Thursday, and Friday

Matthew 26:1–35; Mark 14:1–31; Luke 22:1–38; John 13—17

". . . Jesus knowing that His hour had come that He would depart out of this world to the Father, having loved His own who were in the world, He loved them to the end" (John 13:1).

After the argumentative wars on Tuesday, God gave Jesus a day off. We do not know where He was on Wednesday, with whom He spent that day, or what He did. The silence thunders at us! The Pharisees had rejoiced over the rout of the Sadducees by Jesus, but their humor quickly turned to hatred when Jesus silenced them. His enemies reasoned, "Since we cannot answer Him, we must kill Him."

Jesus may not have been busy on this day, but Judas was. His betrayal was not impulsive—it was deliberate. The Sanhedrin, the Jewish high council, was also busy, meeting in a secret session. Satan, too, was busy. Wednesday was the calm before the storm. Wouldn't you guess that Jesus spent that day in prayer to God?

PREPARING FOR THE PASSOVER
Jesus awoke on Thursday morning never to sleep

again. The "hour" had come. Following a respite on Wednesday, Jesus renewed His march to the cross. He was in charge of what would happen. Others thought they were, but they were not. Jesus initiated and brought about the cross. He was determined, but not in a hurry.

The objective for this day was to prepare the Passover meal (Matthew 26:17–19; Mark 14:12–16; Luke 22:7–13). Jesus told His apostles to find and follow a man carrying a pitcher of water. He would be the only man in Jerusalem doing that, for it was "women's work." The apostles did as Jesus said and found a room prepared. Consider how amazing this is! They needed a large room. The Passover was for a group. Jerusalem was overflowing with people. Surely, there were no empty rooms. Not only was this room empty, but it was also ready! How could this be? God's awesome providence was at work here! God can make impossible things possible in our lives too.

Jesus had a deep interest in eating this Passover with the apostles (Luke 22:14–16). Several reasons can be given: (1) Jesus announced His desire to eat the Passover because of His approaching suffering. He wanted and needed the apostles' companionship. (2) Furthermore, this was to be God's last Passover meal. Jesus nailed the law of Moses to the cross (Colossians 2:14). What God gave, God took away. (3) Jesus is now our continuous Passover (1 Corinthians 5:7). (4) In this situation of eating the Passover in the upper room, Jesus initiated His Supper.

Two things command our attention: (1) the authority of the Scriptures and (2) Jesus' obedience. Jesus kept God's law! He was born, lived, and died under the law of Moses. He obeyed the law of Moses to the letter and in the right spirit (Matthew 5:17–20), but He did not yield to the man-made rules of the Pharisees. *Do not devalue the Scriptures. Oppose false teachers and false teaching in the spirit of love.*

SERVING WITH A TOWEL

We now come to Thursday night, the beginning of the Jewish Friday. As Jesus was about to die, the apostles fussed over who was the greatest (Luke 22:24–30). Could it be that Judas was involved in this? He had led in the tirade against Mary and the anointing that had honored Jesus (John 12:1–8). His spirit displayed the kind of heart he had.

Every group has to have a leader. Someone must be responsible. Jesus designated Peter, James, and John to be His leaders. Could there have been resentment, jealousy, or a power struggle going on among the apostles?

Judas' betrayal of Jesus was no impulsive decision. The seating at the meal could have triggered the outburst, but the problem was far greater. Jesus had taught against the heathen idolatry of power, saying, "It is not this way among you" (Matthew 20:20–28; Mark 10:35–45). James and John (with their mother) had requested special privilege and power. Jesus said much about pushing and shoving for chief seats (see Matthew 23:6–12; Mark 12:38–40; Luke 20:45–47). We have similar problems with pride and arrogance today. We can overcome these by developing the humble attitude displayed by Jesus (Philippians 2:5–8).

How did Jesus handle all that He had to endure? He did not yell, threaten, or harshly rebuke. If we had been in charge in place of Jesus, we would have prayed to God, "We need a whole new group of apostles!" Instead, quietly, He taught and taught! He picked up a towel and washed their feet (see John 13:1–17). The silence was deafening. It was shattered by Peter's outburst: "You will never wash my feet!" Firmly, yet gently, Jesus silenced Peter. It is easier to wash feet than it is to be washed. The Son of God began laying the foundation for His church with a towel. He declared Himself to be "The Servant" (see Luke 22:27). Jesus washed the feet of those who were present, including Judas. He then began the first of many warnings to His apostles, but they were given without success.

IDENTIFYING A BETRAYER

At the Passover meal, Jesus announced the betrayal that was coming. We would probably think it was obvious to the others that Judas would be the betrayer, but that was not the case. The apostles did not believe that any of the others among them would betray the Lord . . . but each was afraid that he himself could (Matthew 26:21–25; Mark 14:18–21; Luke 22:21–23; John 13:21–30). Judas asked, "Is it I?" (Matthew 26:25; NKJV). Jesus told the apostles that His betrayer was the one to whom He would give the "morsel" (John 13:26). When He gave the piece of bread to Judas, amazingly, the other apostles totally missed it. Judas knew that Jesus knew! (See Matthew 26:25.)

Years ago, Reuel Lemmons had a sermon entitled "And It Was Night," based on John 13:30, which says, "So after receiving the morsel [Judas] went out immediately; and it was night." God is light; sin is darkness. Judas left the light for the darkness. Satan's entrance into Judas was not mystical or supernatural. Judas allowed and welcomed him in. *How tragic it is to leave light for darkness!* Judas left before Jesus said the words in John 13:34, 35: "A new commandment I give to you, that you love one another, even as I have loved you, that you also love one another. By this all men will know that you are My disciples, if you have love for one another." Sin does catastrophic harm; part of the tragedy of sin is in what you miss. Judas missed so much! He never saw the risen Lord.

INSTITUTING HIS SUPPER

After Jesus dismissed Judas, He instituted the memorial we call the Lord's Supper (Matthew 26:26–29; Mark 14:22–25; Luke 22:17–20; 1 Corinthians 11:23–26). Read John 6:48–58. This is not a reference to the Lord's Supper, but it is doctrinal truth. To be saved we must ingest Christ—His life, doctrine, and salvation.

The Lord's Supper was initiated in an assembly. The early church assembled to partake of it (Acts 20:7). New Testament worship glories in its simplicity—the bread and a cup.

FINAL DETAILS

Jesus' attention next centered upon Peter, who vowed unlimited allegiance. Jesus stated that before the rooster crowed, Peter would deny Him three times. Read Matthew 26:33–35; Mark 14:29, 30; John 13:36–38. Luke 22:31–34 offers more detail. Satan desired Peter, but Jesus said He had prayed for him. Had Jesus equally prayed for Judas? Surely, He had. Not all our prayers can be answered the way we want them to be!

Little is known about where, when, and how Jesus prayed "The High Priestly Prayer," the real "Lord's Prayer" in John 17. This prayer is perhaps the greatest prayer ever prayed! He prayed for His apostles, Himself, and us!

The cross . . .
there is no other way!

5

Gethsemane

Matthew 26:36–46; Mark 14:32–42;
Luke 22:39–46; John 18:1

"Then Jesus came . . . to a place called Gethsemane . . ."
(Matthew 26:36).

Before going to the cross, Jesus went to Gethsemane, a garden near Jerusalem, to pray about the sacrifice He would make for us. "Gethsemane" simply means "oil press." This garden, across the brook from Jerusalem on Mt. Olivet, was Jesus' "prayer closet" when He was in Jerusalem (John 18:1, 2). The story of His time there is poignant, precious, profound, and priceless!

A time of prayer! It was going to be a long night, and Friday was going to be a long day of agony. He left eight of the apostles at the garden gate, taking Peter, James, and John deeper into the garden. He left these three with the command to "keep watching and praying" as He went on alone (Matthew 26:41; Mark 14:38).

Jesus fully knew His "hour" had come. His metaphorical word for this time was "cup" (see Matthew 26:39; Mark 14:36; Luke 22:42). What was this "cup"? The battle of all eternity was being fought between God and Satan. The winner would take all. Humanity was at stake. Jesus fought to conquer Satan, sin, death, and hell . . . alone! On the cross He would cry, "My God, My God, why have You forsaken Me?" (Matthew 27:46; Mark 15:34). (1) He would be made what God hates—sin. (2) The eternal wrath of God was about to be poured out upon Him. (3) For the only time in all eternity, God the Father and Christ the Son would be separated. Horror of horrors! Nevertheless, Jesus did not want out of this arrangement to save mankind. He was never arrogant in His humanity.

Jesus had already prophesied His imminent betrayal. How disappointed, hurt, and rejected He must have been! Judas would betray Him; Peter would deny Him. Only one of the twelve apostles (John) would even be at the cross. Israel, God's chosen people, would reject Him in favor of a common criminal (Barabbas).

The most dominant ministry of Christ was prayer. If Jesus needed prayer, how much more do we? He invited Peter, James, and John to watch with Him—but they slept. He knelt and then fell face down. As He prayed, He became more and more intense in His appeal to God.

Prayer is not a guarantee that God will grant every wish. Our prayers are always under the will of God. Jesus reminded God that He was the God of the impossible!

Eternal decisions can only be made in prayer. Nothing can be settled until prayer settles it. Jesus had to wrestle in prayer to yield His heart to the sacrifice demanded by God. The prayer He prayed is the most difficult one ever prayed. This was the "Holy of Holies" in the life of Christ. His final teachings were given through these prayers.

God answered Jesus' prayer immediately. An angel came to strengthen Him (Luke 22:43). One angel? *One?* God sent two angels to Mary Magdalene and the women at the empty tomb (Luke 24:1–10; John 20:11, 12). Jesus could have called for twelve legions of angels (Matthew 26:53), but He got *one*? A supernatural miracle could not substitute for human responsibility. No man knew better than Jesus that ". . . the spirit is willing, but the flesh is weak" (Matthew 26:41; Mark 14:38). Only in humanity could sinful man be saved. Jesus, as man, did what no man could do: "In the days of His flesh, He offered up both prayers and supplications with loud crying and tears to the One able to save Him from death, and He was heard because of His piety" (Hebrews 5:7).

Even the cross did not have the anxiety of Gethsemane. The only time in Scripture Jesus called God "Abba" (Aramaic for something similar to "Daddy") was in that garden (Mark 14:36). In Gethsemane Jesus did not hide, run, or even fight . . . He prayed.

A time of decision! Critics suggest a lack of courage on Jesus' part—perhaps even cowardice. This would contradict everything Jesus *is*! Jesus was not a coward. He was not afraid of death, pain, or the cross. He was not asking God to abort the cross. This cross was God's eternal purpose. As the divine Son of God, He was willing to be the ultimate sacrifice for our sins; yet, as a man, He longed for another way. This is part of the mystery of the cross.

Jesus' battle to submit to God's will was won in Gethsemane, before He reached Golgotha.[1] In this garden God said no and Jesus said yes. Jesus accepted the divine judgment and punishment that sin deserves. "It is finished!" was said on the cross, but His decision to submit to God's plan was made in Gethsemane. Jesus gave His soul in the garden and His body on the cross.

---

[1]Golgotha (see John 19:17) is also called "Calvary" (Luke 23:33; KJV), from a Latin word (*calvaria*) which means "skull."

In athletics the game is won through preparation, decision, and commitment. Jesus won the battle in Gethsemane. *Make the big decision before the cross. Don't wait until you are on a cross to decide what you are going to do.*

A time of pain! There must have been more agony in Gethsemane than at Calvary. No man ever suffered as Jesus suffered then. The Scriptures say more about His suffering in Gethsemane than on the cross.

Under severe duress, the "sweat became like drops of blood" (Luke 22:44). He was in an agony unto death. His sweat *did* drop like blood. Such is a rare phenomenon (called hematidrosis or hemohidrosis). He prayed this way not just once, but three times! He prayed, "May this cup pass from Me." His critics were right: "He saved others; He cannot save Himself" (Matthew 27:42; Mark 15:31; see Luke 23:35). God did answer Jesus' prayer! He did not spare Jesus, but He did save us! Jesus could not save Himself and still be our Savior. *There was no way but the cross!*

This God-forsaken Son is the centerpiece of the Christian faith. Do not minimize the physical pain Jesus endured on the cross. It was horrible! However, the Bible refers only sparingly to the pain He suffered. Jesus did not "sweat blood" on the cross. He did in Gethsemane. God sent an angel to the garden to strengthen Him (Luke 22:43). No angel was sent to the cross.

The cross . . .
there is no other way!

6

The Arrest

Matthew 26:47–56; Mark 14:43–52; Luke 22:47–53; John 18:2–12

"While He was still speaking, behold, Judas, one of the twelve, came up accompanied by a large crowd with swords and clubs, who came from the chief priests and elders of the people" (Matthew 26:47).

Judas knew where Jesus would be. He told the Jewish leaders that he would lead them to Him. He knew that Jesus would be praying—but he did not know Jesus!

We know about Jesus, but do we really know Him? How could Judas not know Jesus? How can we not know Him? Is there a "Judas" lurking in all of us? We must read Matthew 26, Mark 14, Luke 22, and John 18 carefully.

The mob led by Judas arrived. Men in a mob lose their individuality. Hatred rejects thought. The armed mob was scared—scared to death of Jesus. They did not deny or doubt that Jesus had raised Lazarus from the dead. In fact, they had considered killing Lazarus too (John 12:10). Judas was their solution; he gave them an opportunity to find Jesus when He was not surrounded by a crowd of followers (Matthew 26:14–16; Mark 14:10, 11; Luke 22:3–5).

How amazing this is! Hundreds came heavily armed to arrest one unarmed prophet. Jesus stood out in the open, saying, "Here I am," and the mob fell back upon the ground! (See John 18:3–6.)

Judas had led this group to Jesus, yet he still called Jesus "Rabbi" (Matthew 26:49). Jesus still called him "friend" (Matthew 26:50). Was this sarcasm? Probably not. Did this aid in Judas' feeling remorse? Probably.

Peter, frightened, resorted to force. He drew his sword and cut off the right ear of Malchus! Peter knew how to use his sword. He knew upon whom he could use it (Malchus, a slave, not an official). He was saying, "You can kill us, but some of you will die too." Jesus told Peter to put away his sword and calmly restored Malchus' ear. (See Matthew 26:51, 52; Mark 14:47; Luke 22:50, 51; John 18:10, 11.)

We must examine the plight of Judas to keep us from his sin (Matthew 27:3–10). He returned the money he had received for betraying Jesus (thirty pieces of silver); it was now worthless to him. The betrayer had remorse that comes from pride, but he did not have repentance that comes from humility. He committed suicide.

Judas could see his mistake, but he could not see his Savior. He went out and hanged himself. No one even cut him down (Acts 1:15–19). Sin has terrible consequences. The traitor "turned aside to go to his own place" (Acts 1:25) and is never mentioned again in the Scriptures. Jesus said that he should never have been born (Matthew 26:24; Mark 14:21)!

The cross . . .
there is no other way!

7

Jesus' Trials

Matthew 26:57—27:31;
Mark 14:53—15:20; Luke 22:54—23:25;
John 18:12—19:16

"For many were giving false testimony against Him, but their testimony was not consistent" (Mark 14:56).

The crucifixion of Christ is so horrible that we tend to overlook or forget other shameless events leading up to it. The trials that Jesus went through were unfair from beginning to end! Jesus was treated so grossly and wickedly that Satan must have blushed! Not even Satan can control sin!

This time of His trials has to be the lowest point in all history. Judas betrayed, Peter denied, ten apostles ran for cover, four puppet rulers—Annas, Caiaphas, Pilate, and Herod—judged the "Judge," and the deeply respected Sanhedrin became a lynch mob. The holiest city (Jerusalem) and the city of law (Rome) united to produce the greatest legal farce in history.

The only one in control was Jesus (John 10:17, 18; 19:10, 11). He had deliberately chosen to go to Jerusalem (Luke 9:51). His "hour" had come (John 17). He forced His enemies to take action by both provoking and facilitating His own arrest. Can we see this?

Today Christ has been reduced to a dear, soft, nice Jesus. No! He was a "man among men," not a glorified weakling. He took on Satan, Judaism, and the whole world—and won. He never retreated from anybody!

Judaism (Jerusalem) was morally and spiritually bankrupt. As we see man at his worst, we also see God in His perfection. This is the glory of grace. Jesus did not sneak into town or hide in a closet. He publicly cleansed the temple (Matthew 21:12, 13; Mark 11:15–17; Luke 19:45, 46). The Jews were so steeped in corruption that they had turned the temple into a cattle auction. Jesus, alone, stopped that. What courage! What strength! Within the city of Jerusalem, He taught "judgment parables." There is no neutrality with Jesus—you either accept Him or put Him on a cross! His enemies never said, "Rebuke Him." They said, "Kill Him!"

The religious leaders were "scared out of their wits" by Jesus! His miracles could not be dismissed. Jerusalem was hostile and unsympathetic to the truth about Jesus. Religious leaders had no control over Him or His ministry.

No one wanted a riot during the Passover. If the Jews had intended to kill Jesus during the feast, they would have made plans and not waited until Thursday night to implement them. This is where Judas entered the scene. Having been with Jesus and listened to His teachings in Jerusalem, he had heard Jesus announce His death. Judas thought that he would make merchandise out of it.

In one sense, Jesus' announcement of His approaching death was good news to His enemies, but the uncertainty that it created during the feast caused them to panic. They had no fear of the fishermen and others who were His disciples, but they did not underestimate Jesus. The Pharisees said, "Look, the world has gone after Him" (John 12:19b). In the eyes of the unbelieving Jews, the resurrection of Lazarus necessitated the death of Christ (John 11). They were afraid that Jesus would convince the whole world!

Such truth as Jesus had given and such miracles as He had worked should terrify sinners! God gave the people of Jerusalem every opportunity to repent, but they refused the evidence. Because of Jesus, the religious leaders were going to lose not only their religious positions, but also their source of monetary gain (John 11:47, 48). No wonder Caiaphas announced that Jesus must die (John 11:49, 50)! "But the Jews were looking for a Messiah," you may say. Yes and no. They talked about it; they exploited it . . . but the last thing the religious leaders wanted was the kind of Messiah that God sent. They knew He would put them "out of business." Pride, with power, does damnable things. Men with pride cannot give up power. They can only reject truth, fight truth, and try to destroy truth. The Jews, out of control, branded Jesus as being "guilty." Pilate pronounced Him "not guilty" (John 18:38).

Among the most obvious irregularities in the trials of Jesus were breaches of the following protocols:

- No decision of guilt or innocence could be made before a trial began.
- Officials had no authority to make an arrest at night unless someone was caught in the act of a crime. Judges were not to be part of an arrest.
- Capital trials could not be held at night.
- A criminal could not be acquitted in one day; a guilty verdict also demanded a night to think about it.

- Crucifixion was unknown to Jewish law.
- The judges were to be defenders as well as accusers.
- Hearsay evidence was inadmissible under Hebrew law.
- Circumstantial evidence was discredited; Hebrew law was based upon two or three witnesses.
- The youngest members of the Sanhedrin were to vote first.
- A member of the Sanhedrin was to be assigned to defend the accused.
- The Sanhedrin had no authority to originate charges . . . only to try them.
- Court sessions were forbidden on feast days and the eve of the Sabbath.
- The accused could not testify against himself.
- A high priest was not to rend his clothes.

Those who were the worst supposed themselves to be the best. It is terrifying to think how monstrous men in sin can be!

THE JEWISH TRIALS

Had it not been so contemptible, the arrest of Jesus would have been comical. The enemies of Jesus believed more in the power of Jesus than the apostles did. They sent a lynch mob (estimated at six hundred or more men) to arrest one man! Jesus, in plain view, had to help them to arrest Him.

Jesus was bounced back and forth like a Ping-Pong ball between the supreme judges. He was first taken to Annas. This high priest had been ordained for life, but his corruption had ousted him. Although he no longer had the title, he was still the man with power.

Annas sent Him to Caiaphas. This shows that Jesus was not on trial for religious reasons, but for the purposes of corrupt politics. Caiaphas, the son-in-law of Annas, was the high priest that year. Annas was powerful, feared, and hated. Caiaphas was but his "errand boy," completely under his control.

Proud, haughty, and conceited beyond words, the Jewish leaders lost their composure. Barbarically, they spat on Jesus, slapped Him, punched Him, cursed Him, and taunted Him to prophesy blindfolded (Matthew 26:67, 68; Mark 14:65; Luke 22:63–65). We can endure curses and slaps maybe, but *spit*? Who can tolerate spit? How did God? Jesus prophesied spit (Mark 10:34; Luke 18:32). His prediction came true. Jewish leaders spat in His face, and Roman soldiers spat on Him (Matthew 26:67; 27:30; Mark 15:19). Disgusting! God's grace can endure anything, including *spit*!

Peter warmed himself by the "devil's fire" (see Mark 14:54; Luke 22:55; John 18:18, 25). In doing this, he placed himself closer to the enemy than to Christ. *Always guard where you are and with whom you are spending your time.*

In quick succession, Peter denied Jesus three times. Then the rooster crowed and Satan exulted. Jesus was being shuffled from trial to trial. As He was moved from Caiaphas to the Sanhedrin, He was taken near the court where Peter was. Jesus turned and looked at Peter, and the apostle's heart melted. He went out and cried over what He had done (Luke 22:61, 62).

The supreme court of the Jews was once praised as the Great Sanhedrin. It was made up of seventy-one august members. Their illustrious position ended that day. Caiaphas, in desperation, forced Jesus to testify against Himself under oath (Matthew 26:62–64). Jesus not only accepted their accusation, but He also gave them further evidence to use against Him: "Nevertheless I tell you, hereafter you will see the Son of Man sitting at the right hand of Power, and coming on the clouds of heaven" (Matthew 26:64). With that, the Jews sent Him to Pilate!

The Jewish leaders were obviously behind the one question that Pilate asked Jesus: "Are You the King of the Jews?" If a charge had not already been made, how did Pilate know what to ask? This suggests that someone had contacted Pilate earlier that night. Who could have gained access to Pilate during the night? Probably, only the high priest, Caiaphas, could have done it. Again, how could the tormenting dream of Pilate's wife make sense (Matthew 27:19)? This explains why the Jewish leaders were insulted when Pilate reopened the case. The Jews thought a deal had been made!

THE ROMAN TRIALS

Pontius Pilate hated the Jews, and they hated him. They were stuck with each other, and each would do anything to win an argument between them. With his record of past mistakes, Pilate had to be very careful. The Jews wanted blood; Pilate wanted to save his political position.

The Jews exchanged the charge of blasphemy for one of political treason. Pilate tried to avoid being part of this travesty, yet he could not. He wanted others to judge, and they refused. He repeatedly declared Jesus "not guilty." In desperation, he sent Jesus to Herod.

Jesus did not acknowledge Herod's request for a magic show. All Herod could do with Jesus was to send him back to Pilate. The only thing achieved by this process was that Pilate and Herod became friends (Luke 23:12).

Pilate marveled at the quiet composure of Jesus. Using Barabbas, he attempted to release Jesus as a favor for the Jews. They rejected it. They chose to free Barabbas, a common thug! People will always choose a Barabbas.

The Jews won yet lost. They declared, "We have no king but Caesar" (John 19:15). They renounced God for Caesar. They bowed to that which they hated, even shouting, "His blood be on us and on our children!" (Matthew 27:25).

Pilate had the "not guilty" Jesus crucified! He had washed his hands; Jesus had washed others' feet. What a difference!

Pilate yielded to the will of the Jews. This was the crime of crimes! Do not be prejudiced like the Jews, amused like Herod, or spineless like Pilate. The historian Eusebius[1] said that Pilate committed suicide. God wiped out Jerusalem (using Titus and the Roman army in A.D. 67–70). Do not mess with God!

The cross . . .
there is no other way!

---

[1] Eusebius *Ecclesiastical History* 2.7.

29

8

Crucifixion

Matthew 27:31-54; Mark 15:20-39; Luke 23:26-47; John 19:17-30

"But He was pierced through for our transgressions, He was crushed for our iniquities; the chastening for our well-being fell upon Him, and by His scourging we are healed" (Isaiah 53:5).

No two words in the English language are more meaningful than "the cross"! We should approach the study of the cross with trembling hearts. It must be a lifelong study for all those who have been saved by it.

Crucifixion! How brutal, barbaric, cruel, and inhumane! Probably, it was invented by Persians and was later perfected by the Romans.

In time, Rome became infamous for its crucifixions. This method of execution was the ultimate form of humiliation. Rome did not crucify Romans. The Jews despised crucifixion (Deuteronomy 21:23; Galatians 3:13); it was never their practice. Animals today are not treated as cruelly as Jesus was.

Modern civilization refuses crucifixion, yet most of the world practices capital punishment. Where capital punishment is practiced today, it is generally done as quickly, painlessly, and humanely as possible.

The scourging! Flogging was a legal preliminary in Roman execution. Jesus prophesied that He would be scourged in connection with His sufferings (Matthew 20:17–19; Mark 10:32–34; Luke 18:31–34), and He was!

Scourging was brutal. It produced great welts, deep stripes, and a swollen body. Often, eyes and teeth were knocked out. Some men died from it. Scourging, however, was not for execution. The whip was for punishment; the nails were for death. Hardened, experienced Roman soldiers knew when to stop. This whipping heightened the pain of crucifixion.

Pilate had Jesus scourged (Matthew 27:26; Mark 15:15; John 19:1), hoping to gain the sympathetic support of the crowd when they saw the lacerated, bleeding Jesus. He said, "Behold, the Man!" (John 19:5). Pilate's ruse did not work. Neither Jesus nor Pilate got any sympathy.

The dying! Crucifixion stripped people of their human dignity. Basically, crucifixion was used to kill a man and yet keep him alive as long as possible. In public view, a man was left naked (for all practical purposes), helpless, and open to abuse. Even with all this pain, men could live for days. Most lived two or three days. What horror! Oddly, there was not a great blood loss. No major arteries were affected. However, it was difficult to breathe. It was harder to exhale than to inhale. A man would push up with his legs to breathe, which increased the pain from the nails. Death resulted primarily from hypovolemic shock and asphyxia exhaustion. When the legs were broken, victims would die within minutes.

The word "excruciating" literally means "out of the cross." Movement on the cross increased one's misery. There was no comfortable position on a cross. The pain was immense. Headaches, burning thirst, spasms of

31

muscles and nerves—the body suffered a million constant shocks.

The wounds! There are five ways a person can be wounded. Jesus absorbed all five. (1) The contused wound involved bruises from fists and blunt instruments (Matthew 26:67; Mark 14:65; Luke 22:63). (2) The lacerated wound came with scourging. (3) The penetrating wound came from the sharp points of the crown of thorns the soldiers crammed upon His head (Matthew 27:29). (4) The perforated wound came when ". . . they pierced [His] hands and [His] feet" (Psalm 22:16). The hands could not bear the weight of the body. The nails went through His wrists, which are part of the hands. (5) The incised wound confirmed that Jesus was dead when a soldier pierced His side with a spear (John 19:34).

The Roman soldiers would not leave the victim until they were sure of his death. The Bible clearly declares that Jesus died on the cross.

Very little emphasis is placed upon the pain and suffering that Jesus experienced. The Scriptures avoid the gruesome details as much as possible. Sinners are saved by Jesus' death, not by His pain. Still, the sufferings were clearly present. The cross was a silent death; victims did not have the strength or the breath to scream. Scourging was called the "little death"; crucifixion was called the "big death."

Study carefully Isaiah 53. Do not allow your heart to become insensitive to the pain of the cross. Never allow yourself to get over the shock of its horror!

The cross . . .
there is no other way!

9

Six Hours, 1

Matthew 27:33–44; Mark 15:22–32;
Luke 23:33–43; John 19:17–27

"When they came to the place called The Skull, there they crucified Him and the criminals, one on the right and the other on the left" (Luke 23:33).

Six hours! Salvation . . . life . . . hope . . . heaven! Jesus was on the cross for six hours (Mark 15:25–37). The third hour until the ninth hour (Jewish time) is equivalent to 9:00 a.m. until 3:00 p.m. These six hours can be equally divided. God divided them. God sent utter darkness from the sixth to the ninth hours (Matthew 27:45; Mark 15:33; Luke 23:44). Jesus died at the ninth hour.

The death of Jesus is the most famous death in history. It is all that Christianity has, wants, or needs. Paul wrote, "For I determined to know nothing among you except Jesus Christ, and Him crucified" (1 Corinthians 2:2). This is the heart of everything that Paul knew and everything that he preached (1 Corinthians 1:17–25).

DETAILS NOT TOLD

We know so little! Details are few. John was the only apostle to witness the crucifixion. Luke (the historian) reduced the cross to one short sentence in one verse: "There they crucified Him" (Luke 23:33b). We know more about His burial than His crucifixion. We have more questions than answers.

We do not know the shape of the cross. The "X"-shaped cross is out of the question. There is also the Tau cross, which looks like our capital "T." Since Pilate had a sign placed above Jesus' head, this, too, is eliminated. The Latin cross, shaped like a plus sign, is probably what was used. It is the universal cross that has been widely accepted and placed in art, jewelry, and architecture. Anecdotally, the plus sign is called "the sign of the cross."

Pilate wrote a sign and placed it above Jesus on the cross (Matthew 27:37; Mark 15:26; Luke 23:38; John 19:19). Each account of it is different, but they all say the same thing. The writers were not interested in the exact words, but in the message that was given through them.

How was Jesus nailed to the cross? We do not know. We know the day Jesus was resurrected: the first day, Sunday (Matthew 28:1–7; Mark 16:2–9; Luke 24:1–7; John 20:1–10). There is no argument here. The early church assembled on that same day of the week (Acts 20:7; 1 Corinthians 16:2).

However, the day of the crucifixion is not named specifically. To find that day, we must count backwards. Ten times the Gospels[1] refer to Jesus' being raised on "the third day."[2] Although the timing is debated, the Bible clearly says the crucifixion day was the preparation day,

---

[1]The Gospels are the first four books of the New Testament: Matthew, Mark, Luke, and John. These books tell the story of the life, ministry, death, and resurrection of Jesus.

[2]See Matthew 16:21; 17:23; 20:19; 27:63; Mark 9:31; 10:34; Luke 9:22; 13:32; 18:33; 24:7.

that is, the day before the Sabbath (Mark 15:42; Luke 23:50–56; John 19:31).

We know how long Jesus was on the cross: six hours. These hours are the wedge in the center of time.

THE FIRST THREE HOURS

Immediately, Jesus was offered vinegar with gall (Matthew 27:34; KJV). Amazing! He rejected it. Jesus refused a painkiller. He did not want anesthetic. He would keep His full senses upon the cross. He would not numb the pain at the price of His faculties. Pain and agony were not issues at the cross. Jesus was the only person at the cross who knew what was taking place.

No sooner was He on the cross than the people chanted for Him to come down (Matthew 27:39–43; Mark 15:29–32; Luke 23:35–37). The thieves joined in also (Matthew 27:44; Mark 15:32; Luke 23:39). What defiant cynicism! This demonstrated the ultimate depravity of unbelief, of disbelief. How dare man tell God the conditions on which he will believe! If Jesus had come down from the cross, sinners would have been condemned and without hope. Jesus was born to die. He died that we might be born to live (Romans 5:10). God, righteous and holy as He is, cannot forgive anyone without punishing the sin. At Calvary, Jesus bore the punishment for our sin.

Even forgiven sins have consequences. In His first statement on the cross, Jesus asked God not to count this sin against His tormentors; however, theirs was the sin of sins! God destroyed Jerusalem. In its biblical history, Judaism existed for one thing—the coming of the Messiah. Jesus came, fulfilling all the prophecies about the Messiah. The Jews crucified Him! Ironically, this put them out of the "Messiah business." They rejected God as their

King, accepting Caesar (John 19:14, 15). They fell further by placing Jesus' blood upon themselves and, to add to their sin, upon their children (Matthew 27:25).

When Jesus spoke again, He addressed the thief next to Him. As Jesus was dying for the sins of all mankind, it was only fitting for Him to forgive a sinner. Study the exchange in Luke 23:39–43. A thief found true religion while being executed. Amazing! Come to the cross, and stay at the cross. The cross saved the thief; the cross can save us! We cannot be saved by ideas, thoughts, philosophies, mysticisms, or ignorance—only Jesus can save us.

Although dying in intense pain, Jesus took care of His mother, Mary. He instructed John to care for her as his mother (John 19:26, 27). Many think John took her into his own home for the rest of her life. Stop and think. Two of her sons later wrote New Testament books (James and Jude). Mary and some of her sons were at the prayer service in the upper room in Jerusalem soon after Jesus' resurrection (Acts 1:13, 14). It is obvious that they would take care of their mother's future needs. Mary needed help *at the cross*—right at the foot of the cross, at the time of the cross! This was her hardest day, her longest night. Jesus was saying, "Stay with My mother!"

Golgotha is ugly. Crucifixion is more ghastly than the cinema could ever picture. God did what only a Father full of love could do. He allowed His Son to bear the divine judgment of sin; He hid His face from His Son.

The cross . . .
there is no other way!

10

Six Hours, 2

Matthew 27:45–54; Mark 15:33–39;
Luke 23:44–47; John 19:28–30

*"Therefore when Jesus had received the sour wine, He
said, 'It is finished!' And He bowed His head and gave up His
spirit" (John 19:30).*

THE FINAL THREE HOURS

Jesus' final three hours on the cross were clothed in
a creepy, unnatural darkness. Quietness ruled. The only
sounds anyone could hear were the groans of three dying
men and the dropping of blood.

In the final three hours, Jesus made four more statements in quick succession. He cried, "Eli, Eli, lama sa-
bachthani?" Interpreted, this means, "My God, My God,
why have You forsaken Me?" (Matthew 27:46; Mark 15:34).
God allowed Jesus to become sin (2 Corinthians 5:21).
Because of this, God and Jesus were separated. How terrifying! Oh, the depth of sin!

Separation from God was a deeper wound upon the
Son of God than any punishment man could inflict. This
statement shouts about man's lostness and his helplessness. Jesus' death not only conquered sin, but it also
conquered death (Hebrews 2:14–18). Christians need not

fear death. Satan is a defeated enemy; sin is a conquered curse. Death has lost its sting (1 Corinthians 15:21–26, 51–58).

Jesus, knowing that God's will was being done, allowed Himself to say, "I thirst." The humanity of Christ is seen in this, His fifth statement. Humanity's deepest cry is "I thirst" (John 19:28, 29; KJV). Cheap wine was handy. Even when something decent was done for Jesus, it was cheap. The "Water of Life" was thirsty! (John 6:51–58). Jesus did not use His deity to cancel out His humanity.

Crucifixion took away all the rights of one's humanity. Isaiah wrote, "But everyone who saw him was even more horrified because he suffered until he no longer looked human" (Isaiah 52:14; CEV). The Jews had looked for the Messiah, but they rejected and crucified Him when He came. What was their hope became their death. Nothing is more empty than a religion without a Messiah.

God does not change. Jesus, the Son of God, depicted what God is like from the cross. After being on the cross for six hours, He made the statement only He could make: "It is finished!" (John 19:30). "The task is done!" Now, God can be just while justifying sinners. Jesus was saying that He had completed everything that the Father had sent Him to do for our salvation. Heaven has to be eternal; it will take us all eternity to begin to comprehend what God did for us. Being with God, we will further understand His glory. Jesus will be there as "The Lamb" (as depicted in the entire Book of Revelation). All eternity will declare what Jesus meant by saying, "It is finished!"

What man could not finish, Jesus did. The mouth of Satan (the accuser) was shut (Revelation 12:9–11). The old law of Moses was nailed to the cross. The new law of

Christ came into effect (Hebrews 8:6–13; 9:12–18; 10:4–14, 18–31). The greatest words ever said were "It is finished!"

Jesus made His last statement on the cross in a loud voice: "'Father, into Your hands I commit My spirit.' Having said this, He breathed His last" (Luke 23:46). Amazing! His crying out took great effort. He wanted all to hear His final words. Notice that He did not commit to God His body or His breath. He committed His spirit. Jesus, God's Son, had chosen to die!

Jesus gave His all for our salvation! His followers should live sacrificial lives too. The church is the only institution on earth that exists primarily for the benefit of those who are not members of it.

THE GLORY OF THE CROSS

Jesus never talked as much about being crucified as He did about being glorified. He said, "Father, the hour has come; glorify Your Son, that the Son may glorify You"; "Now, Father, glorify Me together with Yourself, with the glory which I had with You before the world was" (John 17:1, 5). Our God turned the most inhumane instrument of execution into the greatest motivation! Do not talk about the God "within us" or "beside us" until you grasp the God "above us." God has two thrones—one in the highest heaven and the other in the lowest heart. We do not understand Christ until we understand the cross. The only person worthy of glory gave it all to His Father. Let us not glory in anything but the cross of Christ (Galatians 6:14).

The cross . . .
there is no other way!

11

Statements from the Cross

Matthew 27; Mark 15; Luke 23; John 19

"But Jesus was saying, 'Father, forgive them; for they do not know what they are doing'" (Luke 23:34a).

Nothing reveals God like the cross, and nothing exposes man like crucifixion. The cross is repulsive and grotesque; only God could glorify a death on a cross. Crucifixion was chaos, profanity, agony, pain, and venom.

We would not expect profound philosophy to be on the cross, yet some of the greatest statements in all of history were made from it. Jesus made seven statements while on the cross. The first three focused on others; the final four concerned Himself.

Forgiveness. Jesus first said, "Father, forgive them; for they do not know what they are doing" (Luke 23:34). This was a prayer, not a declaration. Jesus' first and last statements were prayers to His Father.

Jesus desired mercy for His tormentors. However, to receive God's forgiveness, those who crucified Jesus would have to submit to the biblical repentance that leads to reconciliation.

Jesus looked down at those who had nailed Him to the

40

cross and said, "I want you to know God's forgiveness." Prayer was rare on crosses. To pray for the executioners was unthinkable. However, this is what Jesus did. While dying, Jesus prayed for forgiveness for those who were committing the crime of killing God's Son. Some scholars think Jesus repeated this statement throughout His first hours of suffering. The cross is the greatest exhibition of forgiveness that the world has ever known.

Salvation. Jesus said to the thief beside Him, ". . . today you shall be with Me in Paradise" (Luke 23:43). The first statement was for the crowd in general, and the second was for the thief in particular. Jesus promised that the penitent thief would be with Him after he died!

Was this thief more lost than we are? It takes a blood-stained Savior to save sin-soaked sinners! Jesus had power to forgive sin (Matthew 9:6; Mark 2:10; Luke 5:24).

The prophet Isaiah said that Jesus would be numbered with the transgressors (Isaiah 53:12). He was crucified between two thieves.

Responsibility. Jesus said, "Woman, behold your son!" (see John 19:26, 27). The "woman" was Jesus' mother, Mary. John was the "son."

Jesus saw His mother. He forgot His own pain to care for His mother, saying, "John, take care of her." This was not permanent. It was necessary for that day.

Pathos. "My God, My God, why have You forsaken Me?" (Matthew 27:46; Mark 15:34). This is a quotation from Psalm 22:1. From this point on, Jesus' words focused on Himself and the Father.

That moment was the only time in all eternity that God and Jesus were separated. No wonder Jesus was sorrowful "to the point of death" in the garden (Matthew 26:38).

God did not abandon Jesus; He abandoned sin! God forsakes sinners who have forsaken Him. Jesus called upon God twice from the cross. Here, He found that God would be God. To accept us forever, He had to reject His Son temporarily. That is part of the mystery of the cross.

As usual, man missed the point. The people thought Jesus was calling for Elijah! Jesus did not fear nails or death, but He did shudder at the loneliness that came with being made sin. How horrifying that was to Him! Jesus was made everything that sin is to God, and He had to suffer through this awful agony *alone*! He never tried to save Himself. This is the depth of His vicarious death. If He was to save us, He could not save Himself. He could not do both.

Thirst. After six long hours, He said, "I thirst" (John 19:28; KJV). His words fulfilled another Scripture (Psalm 69:21).

Not every statement made by Jesus on the cross was recorded in every Gospel Account. Basically, one writer revealed what the others did not.

Jesus kept His full senses and a clear mind while upon the cross. He first refused a drink that would dull His senses. Here, He requested a drink to keep His senses. He had kept His composure and alertness upon the cross.

Of all the pains and discomforts He experienced upon the cross, thirst is the only one He mentioned. These two words comprise the only physical need that Jesus mentioned from the cross. It was the only personal favor He requested. His short statement is power-packed with thought. Only when He knew He had fulfilled His task (John 19:28) did Jesus ask for water.

Victory. He said, "It is finished!" (John 19:30). It is one word in Greek—*tetelestai*. This is the greatest single word ever said. When we hear this word, we realize how little we know. Only Jesus, with one word, could sum up the entire plan of redemption![1]

It will take all eternity for us to grasp what our salvation means! Jesus is the only person who fully did what God wanted done! He said, *"Tetelestai!"* Jesus came to do God's will. He did it! Man, lost in sin, now has a Savior. *Hallelujah!*

Faith. Jesus said, "Father, into Your hands I commit My spirit" (Luke 23:46). He did not die in doubt. He died in joyous faith!

Yes, man in a human sense killed Jesus, yet in another sense man did not. Jesus chose when He would die and when He would be resurrected. He said, "No one has taken it [My life] away from Me, but I lay it down on My own initiative. I have authority to lay it down, and I have authority to take it up again" (John 10:18). Jesus told Pilate that his power was only allowed by God (John 19:10, 11). The spirit of Jesus was not taken from Him; He voluntarily gave it to the Father.

Think of how Jesus lived! Think of how Jesus died! His final words also fulfilled a Scripture (Psalm 31:5). Jesus, the Word (John 1:1), respected "the Word." We must have the same attitude toward it!

Jesus spoke in triumph!

The cross . . .
there is no other way!

---

[1]God's plan to save mankind from sin (see Hebrews 2:9).

12

Statements to the Cross

Matthew 27; Mark 15;
Luke 23; John 19

"'He saved others; He cannot save Himself. He is the King of Israel; let Him now come down from the cross, and we will believe in Him'" (Matthew 27:42).

Who can forget what Jesus said *from* the cross, and who can appreciate what people said *to* the cross? When we listen to ourselves, we are embarrassed, disappointed, and exasperated by what we hear.

What was said to Jesus when He was on the cross?

Challenge. People said, "If You are the Son of God, come down from the cross" (Matthew 27:39, 40). Jesus' tormentors said, ". . . come down from the cross, so that we may see and believe!" (Mark 15:32). Believing is not at all what they would have done. If Jesus had come down from the cross, they would have put Him back on it! People with demands cannot and will not believe. Stubborn sinners cannot believe. No one could deny that Lazarus had been resurrected by Jesus' power (John 11). However, this resurrection precipitated Christ's death. When we do not want to believe, even miracles cannot help us!

Magic. One of the men being crucified with Christ

44

said, "Are you not the Christ? Save Yourself and us!" (Luke 23:39). "Amaze us with a trick," he was saying. Jesus is not a magician. There is a sense in which no one is as unsensational as God! Men crave excitement. Even those at the cross could not just watch, listen, and learn. They tried to make something happen. Everything they said and did failed. People today promote excitement. They want "holy goose bumps." They hear with their eyes and think with their feelings. The impenitent thief was guilty of many crimes, even blasphemy (Luke 23:39). He called over to the Lord and mockingly asked Him for salvation. How could a dying man be so brazen?

Man is his own worst enemy. What if Jesus had saved Himself? Then man would have been doomed. Jesus stayed on the cross and sacrificed Himself to save us.

Change. One thief was impenitent, but the other said, "Remember me" (Luke 23:42). The cross either makes men better or worse. The selfish life of one thief ended in his selfish death. The other thief repented. He pushed through the circumstances and focused upon Jesus, asking for mercy. This thief was one man on earth who had some understanding of what was happening. He realized that he had lived a wicked life, and he saw the need to change. The gospel message must be "bad news" before it can be "good news."

Gawkers. Others said, "Let us see whether Elijah will come to save Him" (Matthew 27:47–49; see Mark 15:36). Gawkers are dangerous. After Jesus cried aloud to God, bystanders did what bystanders do—they mixed up everything! Hearing a cry from the depths of Jesus' heart, superstitious men confused Elijah with God. Bystanders (thrill-seekers) see everything and observe nothing. They see all that happens and understand little. All that bystanders offered Jesus was vinegar! What a travesty!

Gamblers. The soldiers said of Jesus' tunic, "Let us not tear it, but cast lots for it" (John 19:24). Jesus was dying for our sins while men were gambling for His clothes. Only a hardened man could gamble at the cross.

All of us are selling our lives for something. A man can gain the whole world and lose his soul (Matthew 16:24–26). Men gambled while the Son of God was dying to save them! Men were more interested in the worth of a robe than the life of a man. Things were more important than people. Are we any different? Are we any better? We know the price of everything and the value of nothing. Jesus went back to heaven; the robe soon disappeared. Spiritual values last; temporal things pass away.

Conclusion time. A centurion, observing what had happened, said, "Truly this man was the Son of God" (Mark 15:39). This was just another workday for this war-hardened soldier, but perhaps he took pride in his job and did it well. He watched every movement; he heard every word. Jesus was different; this cross was different. Unknowingly, this honest man immortalized himself. What the world, the crowds, and the enemies totally missed, this man saw! He drew the only conclusion that one can honestly draw. Either Jesus is the Son of God, or He is not! The centurion made his decision; we must make ours!

We all find ourselves at the cross. What a motley group we see there: enemies, the curious, the ignorant, spectators, the scared disciples, and the loved ones! Jesus was the only one who was fully living out God's will.

The cross . . .
there is no other way!

13

Six Miracles
Connected with the Cross

Matthew 27:45–54; Mark 15:33–39;
Luke 23:44–47

"And behold, the veil of the temple was torn in two from top to bottom; and the earth shook and the rocks were split. The tombs were opened, and many bodies of the saints who had fallen asleep were raised" (Matthew 27:51, 52).

God warned the Jews time and time again about rejecting Jesus. There was no excuse for them not to become believers. Jewish leaders knew that Jesus was divine; but, in their hate and blindness, they chose to kill Him. Even Pilate knew who He was and pronounced Him "not guilty" (John 18:38).

Consider what took place before the crucifixion. During the arrest in the garden, when Jesus said, "I am He," many in the mob drew back and fell on the ground (John 18:6). This should have stopped the whole sordid affair!

Then there was the healing of a servant's ear! Peter drew his sword and flicked off Malchus' ear, but Jesus healed it. This was the last miracle for the Jews before Jesus went to the cross. Jesus could manage anything!

We must not forget the miracle that never happened! Jesus said to Peter, "I could ask for legions of angels to help us, but I won't." Read and reread Matthew 26:50–56; Mark 14:46–50; Luke 22:47–53; and John 18:3–12. Jesus used this occasion to present Himself to God as our atoning sacrifice for sin.

Those who do not want to believe, after a time, cannot believe. Why has the world not been convinced by the miracles that happened in connection with the cross?

1. DARKNESS

"When the sixth hour came, darkness fell over the whole land until the ninth hour" (Mark 15:33; see Matthew 27:45; Luke 23:44). Jesus was on the cross six hours. The first three belonged to the crowd; the last three belonged to God! The darkness was a preview of hell (2 Peter 2:4; Jude 6, 13) and a reminder that the One dying was the Son of God.

This darkness was not an eclipse of the sun. An eclipse lasts only a few minutes and cannot happen during a full moon. Passover came during a full moon. The darkness was eerie, providing prevailing quietness, except for the moans of three dying men and the voices of those who were wondering out loud what was happening. The shame of Calvary smothered the sun. Those present could see only darkness.

2. THE VEIL

At 3:00 p.m., Jesus cried with a loud voice. The priests were on duty at the temple. Before their startled eyes, the veil separating the Holy Place from the Holy of Holies tore from top to bottom (Matthew 27:51a; Mark 15:38; Luke 23:45b). God was removing Himself from His earthly temple. As of this moment, the law of Moses was gone; the Levitical priesthood was gone. No wonder many priests later obeyed the gospel (Acts 6:7).

3. THE EARTHQUAKE

At the same time when the veil was torn, "the earth shook and the rocks were split" (Matthew 27:51b). This earthquake brought a suspense that was surely terrifying. Even Roman soldiers were awed at the earthquake (Matthew 27:54). Rocks, some of the hardest substances on earth, were split! Everything shook except the cross!

4. THE OPENED GRAVES

Earlier, the Jews had demanded a sign from Jesus. God gave them six miracles connected with the cross. The splitting of the rocks was brute force; the opening of the graves was brilliant design (Matthew 27:52, 53). What an unusual earthquake! Only selected graves were opened! "And all the crowds who came together for this spectacle, when they observed what had happened, began to return, beating their breasts" (Luke 23:48). God was still teaching, warning, and reaching out to the Jews. This also proves that the events on the Day of Pentecost (the beginning of the church in Acts 2) were no accident. Peter began the first gospel sermon, testifying, ". . . as you yourselves know" (Acts 2:22). Before that occasion, God had given them fifty days to think about the cross. On the Day of Pentecost, Peter gave them the solution to their guilt—Christ.

5. THE GRAVE CLOTHES

After the women told the apostles that Jesus had risen from the dead, Peter and John ran to the tomb to see for themselves. They found only an empty tomb. John looked in and saw evidence of a resurrected Savior: The linen wrappings and face-cloth from Jesus' body were lying there (Luke 24:1–12; John 20:1–9). The last thing the enemies wanted was an empty tomb! Had the disciples been removing His body, they would not have disrobed it. Enemies would not have taken the time to disrobe it. The grave clothes were enough evidence for John. He was the first to believe! (See John 20:8.) We, too, must think logically about this!

6. THE RESURRECTED SAINTS

The graves were opened on Friday (Matthew 27:50–53). The resurrected saints[1] did not walk in Jerusalem until Sunday. To remain ceremonially clean, the Jews could not greet their departed loved ones. What a monumental miracle! What would you have done if you had been there?

These six miracles connected with the cross provide evidence that the One crucified was God's dear Son. They give indisputable proof. Whoever believes the Source, that is, the New Testament writings, has to be convinced by these amazing wonders.

The cross . . .
there is no other way!

---

[1]"Saints" are those set apart for holy living (see 1 Corinthians 1:2). In the New Testament, all Christians are called "saints."

14

People at the Cross

Matthew 27; Mark 15; Luke 23; John 19

"But standing by the cross of Jesus were His mother, and His mother's sister, Mary the wife of Clopas, and Mary Magdalene" (John 19:25b).

Study the Bible reverently and honestly. Try to put the pieces together and see the whole picture that it gives of each divine episode. Be diligent. Clear your heart of all prejudice! Let God tell you what to believe. Do not try to make the Bible say what it has not said.

Our judgment of biblical characters is more a judgment of ourselves. We see ourselves in each one of them. We will find that great teachings come from people at the cross. Equally, great teachings come from people who were *not* at the cross. Keep your eyes wide open. Unanswered questions are not as dangerous as answers to questions that God does not ask.

SOME WHO WERE ABSENT

Judas. Judas was not at the cross. His story is the worst of all human stories! God does not think or act like man. No one demonstrates this more than Judas.

51

His name sends shudders up and down our spines.

Some suggest that God rejected Judas and that is why he betrayed Jesus. This denigrates God. God does not misuse or abuse people. Recent interpretations of this story assign to Judas a lofty cause! "He did what he did because he had a great cause in mind," they say. This cannot be! Jesus chose Judas, Judas chose Jesus, and then Judas chose to betray Jesus.

Jesus allowed Judas to approach Him and even kiss Him (Luke 22:47, 48). Through all of the arrest, Jesus was saying in several different ways, "Don't do this—run, Judas, run."

The only conclusion we can draw from this is that Judas was a successful hypocrite. The other eleven apostles would have stopped him if they had understood what he was about to do. They did not know his heart by his outward appearance. He had no horns or pitchfork. Jesus knew that Judas had allowed the devil to enter his heart, and He called him the "son of perdition" (John 17:12). John 12:4–6 says that Judas, the trusted treasurer, was a crook and had stolen from the apostles' money bag.

Satan "entered" Judas (Luke 22:3; John 13:27). A man who is made for God, if the man allows it, can be used by Satan. Jesus told Judas as he moved toward his terrible deed to "act quickly" (John 13:26–30). As a disciple, he was disloyal to his teacher. He betrayed Jesus for only a few dollars.

Few men were as blessed as Judas. He was with Jesus for three years. He had special privileges, yet he failed to benefit from them. He could not learn; he could not admit error; he could not repent. To be blunt, Judas could not accept Jesus' grace. Judas had regret from pride, not repentance through grace.

No man was ever warned as Judas was. Months before the betrayal, Jesus said, "Did I Myself not choose you, the twelve, and yet one of you is a devil?" (John 6:70). Judas may have thought that he could be forgiven, but that there was no way he could be restored as an apostle. "My brethren could never forgive me and accept me after this," he may have said to himself. Judas feared life more than death. He committed suicide—a permanent solution to a temporary problem. If Jesus could not save all those close to Him, neither can we!

The other apostles. Eleven of the twelve apostles are not seen at the cross. Judas had killed himself, and ten did not show up. Only John went the entire distance . . . and yet we have no record of him saying anything at the cross. Jesus deserved better! Would we have done better?

Even though they did not show up at the cross, Jesus still forgave and used the apostles. This gives us hope! The apostles simply fled (Matthew 26:56; Mark 14:50; see Zechariah 13:7). Faith believes that God knows what He is doing! Was the cross too much for the apostles? Did the pain and agony overcome them? The Bible does not stress the suffering that Jesus bore. It emphasizes the value of the blood, the death for our salvation, and the resurrection.

Mary, Martha, and Lazarus. These three are not specifically mentioned as being at the cross, at the tomb, or in the upper room (see, for example, Matthew 27:55, 56, 61; Mark 15:40, 47; Luke 23:49, 55; 24:10; John 19:25; Acts 1:13, 14). They are not listed in Acts or in the Epistles.[1]

---

[1]The Epistles are the twenty-one books in the New Testament which were originally written as letters to Christians. They contain valuable teaching on how to live the Christian life.

These were the people with whom Jesus spent His final days. He loved them (John 11:5).

Many times, you have the least influence over those you love and those to whom you devote the most effort. Had these three already been hurt too much (John 11:1–44)? It has been noted that the resurrection of Lazarus precipitated the crucifixion of Jesus. Did they think their lives would be in danger if they stood at the foot of the cross? Was it too risky for them to stay with Jesus?

Others. Were the physical brothers of Jesus there? They were in the upper room in Acts 1, but they were not at their mother's side at the cross. John stood there, but they didn't (John 19:25–27).

Was Barabbas there? We would call him a terrorist (Mark 15:7; Luke 23:18, 19). Pilate was shocked that the Jews chose to release Barabbas rather than Jesus (Matthew 27:15–23; Mark 15:6–14; Luke 23:17–23). What do you think Barabbas should have done?

What about the many people Jesus had healed? Were they there? Were they too embarrassed or too ashamed to be present?

SOME WHO WERE PRESENT

Simon of Cyrene. When the humanity of Jesus failed, Simon was there. Jesus could carry His cross no farther, so the procession to Golgotha was interrupted (Matthew 27:32; Mark 15:21; Luke 23:26).

We usually try to avoid interruptions. Some can be painful. We often think, "After this interruption, we can get back to life." No, no, no! Life is nothing but interruptions. The Gospels tell us about many interruptions in the life of Christ. On this occasion, Simon's life was interrupted too.

Simon was told to carry Jesus' cross. Here is God's providence! This man had traveled hundreds of miles on the religious pilgrimage of a lifetime. Suddenly, he was commandeered to carry a prisoner's cross.

Mark inserted an interesting parenthetical note. Simon, he said, was the father of Alexander and Rufus (Mark 15:21). He may have been the father of the Rufus whom Paul mentioned in Romans 16:13, but we cannot be sure.

Simon had no idea he would still be known today after two thousand years. Whatever his thoughts and motives were, his name will forever be in the Bible and in history. We owe Simon a debt of thanks for carrying the cross when Jesus could barely stand. The part of the cross Simon carried was the crossbeam (crossbar). Thank you, Simon. God always blesses those who assist His Son.

The women. Sympathetic, heartbroken women (Luke 23:27–31) wept for Jesus as He made His way to Golgotha. Jesus gave a frightening revelation to them. They were soon to cry for themselves. Jerusalem crucified Jesus, but God would allow Jerusalem to be destroyed by Roman conquerors (A.D. 67–70).

The women were there. They did not run. They cared. They looked on with deep feelings and emotion. Later, women helped with Jesus' burial and watched His tomb (Matthew 27:55-61; Mark 15:40–47; Luke 23:49–56). May God bless good women who love Jesus!

Mary, the mother of Jesus, was standing sorrowfully by the cross. We are not surprised that she was there. Of all people, who will be with you, no matter what? Your mother! Friends like Peter deny and scatter, but good mothers will always be there! Jesus could not abort His cross; Mary could not abandon her son. She did not fully understand what He was doing, but she was at the foot of the cross.

Every Jewish girl prayed to be the mother of the Messiah. Mary must have been thrilled that God had chosen her to bear and rear His Son (Luke 1:26–38). She also must have been intimidated by the challenge. This was God's only begotten Son! What was it like to rear Him? Mary paid a tremendous price to be Jesus' mother. Simeon, the prophet, had said, "A sword will pierce even your own soul" (Luke 2:35). Only a mother can begin to imagine how Mary felt. Mary lovingly paid the price to rear Jesus. Discipleship will cost us as well. We, too, must be willing to pay the price.

Can we remotely grasp what it was like to live in the house with Jesus? It is easier to grasp His deity than His humanity. Humanly speaking, we might think that Jesus would have been an "A" student, a star athlete, the young man voted "most likely to succeed." Mary must have wondered, "What kind of person will this child turn out to be?" (see Luke 1:66). What an experience she must have had in rearing Him!

What is the lesson here? In spiritual matters, the physical family does not count. God is not partial (Acts 10:34). There was no fanfare for the family of Jesus. Mary, Jesus' brothers, and His sisters had to obey the gospel as others did! They had to become followers of the Christ as all do, and they did. They were present in the prayer session before the first gospel sermon was preached (Acts 1:13, 14). Joseph, the adopted father, was faithful in what he was asked to do. Mary was faithful to her Son and, later, to His church.

Mary, in hearts today, is either banished or deified. Both views are wrong. She did not receive a divinely privileged position, but she was greatly blessed (see Luke 11:27, 28): Her Son became her Savior! (See Acts 1:14.) After the Book of Acts, Mary drops out of the Scriptures.

Other women who loved Jesus were at the cross. Mary Magdalene was there. Jesus, after His resurrection, appeared first to Mary Magdalene, from whom He had cast out seven demons (Mark 16:9; Luke 8:2). There was a third Mary, the mother of James and Joses (Mark 15:40). Also, Salome, the mother of James and John, was there, as was Joanna (Luke 24:10). The women from Galilee (Matthew 27:55; Mark 15:40, 41; Luke 23:49, 55) were there and stayed near the cross. Women were the last ones at the cross and the first ones at the tomb. Praise God for good women!

The thief on the cross. Read Luke 23:39–43. The thief fascinates us. Nothing exposes how we think like this thief. Are we willing to think and be intellectually honest?

The thief was saved. Jesus died *with* sinners *for* sinners. While on earth, He had the power to forgive sin (Matthew 9:4–6; Mark 2:8–11; Luke 5:22–24). He was dying, but He was not dead—and He gave salvation to this man.

Some cry, "The thief was too bad, too fallen, too late, and too far gone." Let us not tell God how to dispense His grace! Let us not tell Jesus whom He can save! Why try to keep any sinner lost? Just think: The greatest day in this thief's life was the day of his crucifixion!

"But he did nothing," you say. Oh, but he did! He claimed the moment. He did what he could. He confessed Jesus as Lord. He rebuked the impenitent thief. He was the only person who defended Christ on the cross.

"He was saved without baptism," you say. Maybe and maybe not! The circumstances suggest that the thief *could* have been baptized. "All Judea" obeyed John the Baptist's baptism (Matthew 3:4–6; Mark 1:4, 5). Religious folk rejected both John and his baptism (Luke 7:29, 30). Publicans and harlots accepted John's baptism. Jesus and His apostles, later, were baptizing more people than John was (John 4:1, 2). Do not gamble your soul upon a thief who may not have been baptized. Never draw an eternal conclusion from an assumption that cannot be settled by revelation.

The thief died under the law of Moses, but we live under the law of Christ (Galatians 6:2). When the thief died, Jesus had not been raised from the dead; He had not given His Great Commission (Matthew 28:18–20; Mark 16:15, 16). At this time, the Holy Spirit had not come; people had not been commanded to be baptized to become Christians. The church had not been established. (That happened on the Day of Pentecost; see Acts 2.) No one can be saved today as the thief was!

Under severe humiliation and excruciating pain, the thief did his best thinking. He rebuked the other thief for blasphemy. He confessed their guilt. He defended Jesus. He used "kingdom language." To some degree, he glimpsed the resurrection. Both the thief and Jesus were dying. Only a great miracle or a resurrection could offer any future hope to him. He did not try to manipulate Jesus as the other thief did. In his helplessness, he threw himself down before "the mercy of the court." This in no way authorizes "deathbed salvation." The thief confessed his faith in Jesus, and he who deserved hell got heaven. The cross shouted to the thief as it shouts to us: "Life is not futile . . . failure is not fatal . . . death is not final!"

The crowds. Gawkers walked by, watching and ridiculing those being crucified (Matthew 26:65–68; 27:47–49;

Mark 14:65; 15:29–36). Crosses brought out the inhumanity in man. To spectators, this was a sport—an ugly, bloody game. Experiments were encouraged: "Come down . . ."; "Stay put . . ."; "Give Him some cheap vinegar . . ."; "Maybe Elijah will come!" What a show! Today, the world is filled with protesters. Where were the protesters when they were needed? "His blood shall be on us and on our children!" the crowd had cried (Matthew 27:25). What a terrible price to pay for the conviction that they got!

The enemies. With pride they said, "We took care of that!" However, Sunday came. They had set their own trap. After the resurrection, Christianity stormed throughout the world. Biblical Judaism ended. Jerusalem was sacked in A.D. 70. What is the point? Simply this: No one can fight against God and win.

Roman soldiers. The soldiers dressed Jesus as royalty and then had a mocking party (Matthew 20:17–19; 27:27–31; Mark 10:32–34; 15:16–20; Luke 18:31–34; 23:11; John 19:1–5). Jesus was beaten severely. The soldiers gambled for His clothes (Matthew 27:35; Mark 15:24; John 19:23, 24). This added insult to injury. However, one Roman centurion watched intently. He saw that Jesus was different. He concluded, as we all must, "Truly this was the Son of God!" (Matthew 27:54; see Mark 15:39; Luke 23:47).

Joseph of Arimathea and Nicodemus. Joseph of Arimathea and Nicodemus asked boldly for Christ's body (Matthew 27:57–61; Mark 15:42–47; Luke 23:50–56; John 19:38–42). We do appreciate them, for they buried Jesus.

Too many people think the way these two men did. Too many only want to serve God in an advisory capacity. Two men who could have done so much did so little! They only claimed the dead body of a man they had secretly believed in when He was alive. Jesus asks us for our lives; sometimes we are only willing to perfume His body! We are not told what became of Joseph and Nicodemus. Their action did take nerve, but it takes true courage to confess Jesus, to make Jesus who He is—Lord.

Some will do more for a lost cause than for a living hope. It is easier to bury the dead than to obey the living Lord.

The cross . . .
there is no other way!

15
Jesus' Death

Matthew 27:50; Mark 15:37;
Luke 23:46; John 19:30

"And Jesus, crying out with a loud voice, said, 'Father, into Your hands I commit My spirit.' Having said this, He breathed His last" (Luke 23:46).

What does Christianity have that other religions do not and cannot have? Jesus Christ and His cross! God cannot and will not save man apart from Jesus' sacrifice for our sins. For those who live in Christ, the judgment has been solved. To those outside salvation, the judgment is yet to come.

Some speak of "cheap grace," but there is no "cheap grace." Grace does not overlook, forget, or repeal God's wrath. Grace absorbs the price, penalty, and punishment for sin. Every sinner and every sin is punished—either in Christ or in hell. Everything of God is in Christ; no spiritual blessings are found outside of Christ (Ephesians 1:3).

JESUS DIED

God, being God, cannot die—yet Jesus died! Concerning His death, we must know *that* He died and *why* He died (for our sins). Too often the focus is only on *how* He died.

We know that Pilate was shocked at how quickly Jesus died (Mark 15:44). Still, he did not doubt that He was dead. The other two being crucified with Jesus had to have their legs broken to speed their deaths (John 19:31–34). Since the Holy Spirit inspired the Gospel writer to include this information, He must have thought it was important for us to know. He wanted us to be sure that Jesus actually died.

Some think Jesus died from exhaustion. He had been deprived of sleep, barely fed, and brutalized in both Jewish and Roman trials. One scholar concluded that Jesus had walked 2.6 miles during these trials. Do not forget the harsh scourging. Exhausted, Jesus was unable to carry His cross.

Others think Jesus died from a broken heart. He was physically depleted and emotionally drained. Jesus was receiving God's holy anger poured out upon Him. One apostle had betrayed Him, another apostle had denied Him, and the remaining apostles, with the exception of John, had deserted Him. Humanly speaking, Jesus had been left alone. "He came to His own, and those who were His own did not receive Him" (John 1:11).

Still others think Jesus died from a ruptured heart. His quick death seems to indicate a catastrophic terminal event.

Few men were more mistreated than Jesus. Whether He died of cardiac rupture or of cardiopulmonary failure, the vital fact is *that* He died, not *how* He died. Roman guards did not leave their victims until they were certain death had occurred. Indeed, Jesus died!

JESUS DIED FOR ME

The Bible never says that Christ lived for us or worked for us, but the Bible emphatically declares that Jesus died for us. Isaiah said He was crushed for our iniquities (Isaiah 53:5). The cross provides God's answer to the problem of sin.

Pilate would not have released the body for burial unless he was certain Jesus was dead (Matthew 15:44–47). He never doubted that Jesus was dead. Jesus' death is historical (abstract). Jesus' death for me is personal (salvational). It is not enough to believe that Jesus died; I must believe that Jesus died for me! Everything Jesus did on the cross, He did for me! God loves me and wants me (John 3:16)! Sing it. . . . Shout it. . . . "I have a Savior!"

Remember this: Preach the gospel to yourself every day. It took a cross to save you; it takes a cross to keep you saved. Ponder the sovereignty of grace.

> You cannot earn grace—it is a gift.
> You cannot buy grace   it is not for sale.
> You cannot merit grace—it is unmerited.
> You cannot repay grace—it creates no debt.
> Grace changes everything—it brings salvation!

Jesus died for my sins (1 Corinthians 15:1–4)! A little girl heard a sermon about the cross. She told the preacher, "You must love Him more than anything else in the world, since He's done all that for you." Yes, we do!

Unmerited love is not unconditional; sinners cannot be saved remaining in the "far country" (Luke 15; KJV). Salvation is not by works of merit, yet Christian love is expressed in good works (Ephesians 2:8–10). Authentic love makes demands; its conditions are not for the childish. Christianity is a gift, not a bargain. It cost Jesus His life; it will cost us ours. Grace is not a genie in a bottle; grace is a cross. Discipleship comes with an awesome price—your life. Jesus' concern on the cross was not for Himself, and we are to follow this selfless example.

Who crucified Christ? I did! Who nailed Jesus to the cross? I did! We cannot understand what Christ did for us until we grasp what we did to cause it! Sin is spiritual rebellion. It is heinous and separates us from God (Isaiah 59:1–3). Christ did for us what we could not do for ourselves. Apart from Christ, we can only die in our sins. Peter accused his audience of murdering Christ (Acts 2:22–36). They had done that physically; we have done it spiritually. We must grasp the depth of sin to accept the glory of grace. If people have not been converted to Christ, they may think they have tried Christianity and failed; in reality, they have not tried it at all. To give yourself and your children a future, give them the cross. The crucifixion explains the creation of the world, our present life, and our future. We should remind ourselves, "Because of me it had to be."

The cross . . .
there is no other way!

16

Jesus' Resurrection

Matthew 28; Mark 16; Luke 24; John 20; 21

"The angel said to the women, 'Do not be afraid; for I know that you are looking for Jesus who has been crucified. He is not here, for He has risen. . . . Go quickly and tell His disciples that He has risen from the dead . . .'" (Matthew 28:5–7).

On Sunday the tomb was empty. An angel asked, "Why do you seek the living One among the dead? He is not here, but He has risen" (Luke 24:5b, 6a). If there had been no empty tomb, the world would never have heard of Jesus. The resurrection is the defining difference that sets Christianity apart from all other religions!

Jesus was not resuscitated, reincarnated, or recreated; He was resurrected. He went "through death and out the other side into a new world, a world of new and deathless creation, still physical only somehow transformed."[1] Christianity claims that something happened to Jesus that had not happened to anyone else in history. Our Christian hope is not just immortality of the soul, but the resurrection and transformation of our bodies.

---

[1] N. T. (Tom) Wright, *Luke for Everyone* (Louisville, Ky.: Westminster John Knox Press, 2004), 296–97.

Most religions have holy places; Christianity does not. Other religions have tombs; Christianity does not. Of what use is a "dead Savior"?

No man witnessed the resurrection. Who *was* there? Was God there? God did resurrect Jesus.[2] Was the Holy Spirit there? Paul said that the Spirit raised Jesus (Romans 8:10, 11). Were angels there? We do not know. Man was not! Christians believe Jesus is the Son of God because of an empty tomb! Christianity would be totally destroyed if one bone of His body were found. Paul said, "That I may know Him and the power of His resurrection" (Philippians 3:10a). Jesus physically died and literally was resurrected. This means that He is alive today. It also means that we can believe in and obey Him today. This is the gospel message! The Christian hope is not life after death, but life, *period*! He said, "I am the resurrection and the life . . ." (John 11:25, 26); "I am the way, and the truth, and the life" (John 14:6a).

The resurrection is without meaning unless it really happened. Jesus is not a liar, a hoax, or a fraud. The cross is not fiction; it is not a myth or an allegory. His death, burial, and resurrection were real. Jesus is historical. Christians do not have a cemetery or a tomb because Christ's tomb is empty. No one denied that His tomb was empty!

THE BURIAL

If Satan ever had a banquet in hell, it was on this Passover Sabbath when Jesus was a corpse. Jesus' resurrection would bring to an end the devil's mirth and release heavenly joy worldwide, throughout eternity.

---

[2]See Acts 2:24, 32; 3:15, 26; 4:10; 5:30; 10:40; 13:30, 33, 34; 17:31; Romans 10:9; 1 Corinthians 6:14; 2 Corinthians 4:14; Galatians 1:1; Ephesians 1:20.

The gospel message is the death, *burial*, and resurrection of Christ (1 Corinthians 15:1–4). We must not think about the death and the resurrection but skip the burial. A burial demands a death. Skeptics tell the fairy tale that Jesus fainted or was in a coma, that He fooled the authorities. Angels pointed out where Jesus' corpse was placed (Matthew 28:6; Mark 16:6). Resurrection demands a death and a burial. A burial demands a body.

The burial shouted, "All is lost. Death has won; life has lost." The situation may have seemed bleak on Friday, but the resurrection came on Sunday!

Jesus did not have a "pre-planned funeral." Neither His family nor His apostles buried Him. Let us marvel at God's providence! Christ died as a pauper, but He was buried as a king! Joseph of Arimathea and Nicodemus, aided by some women, wrapped Jesus' body with linen and expensive spices and buried Him in a new tomb (Matthew 27:57–61; Mark 15:42–47; Luke 23:50–56; John 19:38–42). God takes care of His own!

You only bury those who are dead. Pilate, Joseph, Nicodemus, and the women knew that He was dead. The most basic and certified fact about Jesus is His death.

THE THREE DAYS

Counting back three days from Sunday, the day of the resurrection, some people calculate that Jesus was crucified on Wednesday. Going back that far in the week interferes with Jesus' final activities as recorded in the Gospels. The Thursday theory also creates more problems than it claims to solve. The Bible teaches that He was raised on "the third day"—not "the fourth day" or "the fifth day." Throughout the centuries, Friday has been viewed as the day of His death. Some even call it "Good Friday."

Jesus did speak of three days and three nights in relation to Jonah (Matthew 12:40)—but this was figurative, not
literal. If He had spent three full days and nights in the
tomb, the resurrection would have been on "the fourth" or
"the fifth" day. Man counts hours; the Bible simply refers
to "the third day." From Friday, Sunday is the third day, according to Jewish counting. The Jewish leaders knew this
(Matthew 27:63). They asked Pilate to take action because
they knew what Jesus had said. The apostles remembered
this after His resurrection (Luke 24:8; John 2:18–22). They
then understood what Jesus meant.

Unlike the gentle Jesus we have created in our minds,
Jesus spoke harshly about Herod: "Go, tell that fox, 'Behold, I cast out demons and perform cures today and
tomorrow, and *the third day* I reach My goal'" (Luke 13:32;
emphasis mine). He indeed reached His goal on the third
day—Sunday, the day He rose from the dead!

INFALLIBLE PROOFS OF THE RESURRECTION

"To these He also presented Himself alive after His
suffering, by many convincing proofs, appearing to them
over a period of forty days and speaking of the things
concerning the kingdom of God" (Acts 1:3). Christianity
is built upon tangible, reliable evidence. If Jesus cannot
do anything about death, then whatever else He does
amounts to nothing. The Book of Acts does not debate the
resurrection—it declares it! A dead Savior did not produce
Christianity. Lyman Abbott said, "The resurrection of
Jesus Christ is the best attested fact in history."[3]

Jewish law refused circumstantial evidence. Verdicts

---

[3]Lyman Abbott, *The Theology of an Evolutionist* (New York: Outlook
Co., 1925), 129.

were based on two or more witnesses (2 Corinthians 13:1). God gave considerable space in the Scriptures to the witnesses. The resurrection will stand in any court of law.

(1) *The enemies*. Paradoxically, enemies believed when the disciples doubted. They warned Pilate that Jesus promised a resurrection in three days. Pilate said, ". . . make [the tomb] as secure as you know how" (Matthew 27:65). A huge stone was rolled over the entrance and sealed. Soldiers were put in place to guard the tomb. Humanly speaking, man could not have removed the body.

When the women found the rock rolled aside, exposing the empty tomb, no one shouted, "Find that body!" No one went from house to house in search of the body. Jesus' enemies knew that a corpse could not be found! The rock at the tomb was not rolled aside to allow Jesus to exit, but to allow man to enter. The Jewish leaders, Pharisees, Roman soldiers, Pilate, and Herod were powerless to do anything. They knew Jesus was resurrected! They immediately tried to squelch the news.

Throughout history no one has found Jesus' body. The silence is staggering! Disposing of a human body without a trace would have been a miracle in itself. When Peter preached the first gospel sermon (Acts 2), he was in close proximity to that cemetery. Three thousand people obeyed his message. He told them, "Therefore let all the house of Israel know for certain that God has made Him both Lord and Christ—this Jesus whom you crucified" (Acts 2:36). Skeptics have to face this question: "What happened to that body?"

(2) *The women*. The resurrected Jesus appeared first to Mary Magdalene (Mark 16:9; John 20:1–18). The women came to visit a grave. Honor them for this! Their testimony is made stronger when you realize that they never dared

to imagine a resurrection. When they found the apostles, the apostles laughed at them and refused to believe (Mark 16:10, 11; Luke 24:11). Jesus rebuked the apostles for this (Mark 16:14). They were so focused upon finding a dead body that they could not recognize a living Savior!

(3) *John*. John arrived at the tomb, stopped, and then followed Peter inside. When he saw the grave clothes, he put all the evidence together. He saw and believed (John 20:2–8).

(4) *The apostles*. Cowards became martyrs! What can explain this? The resurrection! Matthew, Mark, Luke, John, Peter, and Paul were competent witnesses. Would you brand them liars? Can you trust the Gospel Accounts in the Bible? Scholars call Luke an historian of the first rank. How can you explain the beginning, the growth, and the continued existence of the early church? It all arises from the resurrection!

(5) *"Doubting" Thomas*. Like the others, Thomas was devastated by the death of Jesus. He missed the first assembly (see John 20:24–29). This failure could have been fatal to his soul. The disciples went after him. We must learn and practice this today (Galatians 6:1, 2; James 5:19, 20; Jude 22, 23). He was present the next time. Do not be too harsh with him. Have you ever seen a resurrected man? Would you believe such a claim? Thomas demanded the "finger test." Jesus welcomed it! Thomas declared, "My Lord and my God!"

(6) *The apostle Paul*. The later conversion of Saul (Paul) is enough to certify the resurrection. Read his story in Acts 9 and 22. The persecutor became the preacher! Why? He saw the risen Savior (1 Corinthians 9:1; 15:8). He had no doubts. He died for his faith and for his preaching. Paul believed in and preached a bodily resurrection.

(7) *The appearances.* Most scholars list ten resurrection appearances, while some list twelve:

- to Mary Magdalene (Mark 16:9–11; see John 20:1–18)
- to other women (Matthew 28:1–10)
- to Simon Peter (Luke 24:34)
- to two men on the Emmaus Road (Luke 24:13–32; see Mark 16:12)
- to ten apostles, without Thomas (John 20:19–25; see Mark 16:14; Luke 24:36–49)
- to eleven apostles, with Thomas (John 20:26–29)
- to seven disciples at the Sea of Galilee (John 21:1–23)
- to eleven apostles in Galilee (Matthew 28:16–20; see Mark 16:15–18)
- to more than five hundred brethren (1 Corinthians 15:6)
- to James (1 Corinthians 15:7)
- to eleven apostles (Luke 24:50–53)
- to Paul (1 Corinthians 15:8; see Acts 9; 26).

Notice that Jesus did not appear before His enemies—the religious Jews, Pilate, or Herod. He appeared to His disciples.

The witnesses have spoken!

IRONIC EPISODES

The Bible is a fascinating book. Mankind could not have written it. We would not have written it if we could have. This fact is a powerful argument for inspiration.

(1) *The women.* The angels and Jesus appeared to women first! The women came with spices. This was a beautiful gesture, but not a practical one. Then it occurred to them: Who would roll away the rock? Several strong

men would have been needed, but it only required one angel!

(2) *The soldiers.* Can there be anything more ludicrous than a group of soldiers guarding a tomb? There was an earthquake; then an angel rolled back the stone (Matthew 28:2). The guards became as dead men. Were they rebuked? Were they commanded, "Find that body"? No! The chief priests bribed the soldiers at a great price to say that they had fallen asleep (Matthew 28:11–15)! The price paid by a soldier found asleep on his watch was always severe—but not in this case!

(3) *The disciples on the Emmaus Road.* Jesus joined two devastated disciples as they walked along the road (Luke 24:13–32). They were amazed that Jesus had "missed" everything that had been happening in Jerusalem. They were the ones who had missed it! Ironically, Jesus, using the Scriptures, preached the gospel to them. They did not recognize Jesus until He blessed and broke the bread.

RESURRECTION POWER

The same power that raised Jesus from the dead can give sinners a new life. This new life begins with baptism into the death, burial, and resurrection of Christ (Romans 6:3–7). A sinner's greatest privilege is to be buried by baptism with Christ and into Christ!

Paul said, ". . . that I may know Him and the power of His resurrection" (see Philippians 3:7–11). The heart and soul of the church is to seek and save the lost. This is done through the power of the gospel, the message of the risen Lord. The cross was the victory won; the resurrection was the sacrificial death accepted, validated, and endorsed by God. Death could not hold Jesus (Acts 2:22–36). In death Jesus defeated and abolished death (2 Timothy 1:10). The cross marks the "death of death." Jesus took the power of death from Satan; He freed us from the "sting" of death (1 Corinthians 15:54–57). Sinners are saved by Christ's death—not by His resurrection.

By His death, Jesus saved us from the law of sin and death (Romans 8:1, 2). To conquer sin is to eliminate death. Jesus appeared in heaven with His blood (Hebrews 10). He is "the resurrection and the life" (John 11:25, 26), not merely "immortality and life." Hell is immortal. Our souls are immortal. Jesus is eternal "resurrection"! Paul promised our change (1 Corinthians 15:50–58). If Christ is not risen, then our faith is empty (1 Corinthians 15:12–19).

Jesus' resurrection guarantees ours. What God did in a Jerusalem cemetery for Jesus, He will do for us. We were not made to die, but to live. What is the doctrine, the hope of the resurrection, *right now*? My life is not futile; it has a purpose. My failures are not fatal; they are forgiven. My death is not final; there is a resurrection. What a hope! We will be like Jesus! When He was on the cross, Satan was defeated, sin was overcome, and death was abolished. "But thanks be to God, who gives us the victory through our Lord Jesus Christ" (1 Corinthians 15:57).

The cross . . .
there is no other way!

17

The Day of Pentecost

Acts 2

"So then, those who had received his word were baptized; and that day there were added about three thousand souls" (Acts 2:41).

How can we explain what happened on the Day of Pentecost (Acts 2)? Three thousand baptisms took place on that day, involving people from all over the known world. How amazing! The speaker, Peter, was an unknown preacher who was not even a rabbi. He did not know what he was going to say to the crowd. The Holy Spirit put the right words in his mouth. He explained who Jesus was and what He had done. This was the greatest response to a sermon in all of history. The most marvelous thing ever produced, the church, was accomplished through the cross and this preaching.

God left nothing to chance. He put it all together. Thousands of Jews had come to Jerusalem for the Passover. For many, this was a major religious pilgrimage, maybe a once-in-a-lifetime experience. Some of these people remained in Jerusalem for *fifty days* until the Day of Pentecost. These people were crowded close together. They could not stop talking about the Passover, the cross, and the empty tomb.

There had never been a Passover like this one! God gave Israel fifty days to think about what had happened. Earthquakes had "rattled their teeth" (see Matthew 27:51–53). From the sixth hour to the ninth hour, the land had been covered in darkness (Matthew 27:45; Mark 15:33; Luke 23:44). God allowed the people to crucify Jesus, but He refused to let them enjoy seeing Him die. This time from 12 noon to 3 p.m. was spooky, weird, and scary! People were too bewildered to move, too afraid not to move.

"What have we done?" was the question. Rocks were rent. Tombs were opened. Recognized folk from these opened tombs walked around after the resurrection (Matthew 27:51, 52). As priests in the temple were serving (at the ninth hour), the veil was torn from top to bottom (Matthew 27:51; Mark 15:38; Luke 23:45b). The frenzy that cried, "Crucify Him!" turned into hysteria. The participants were so disturbed that they smote their breasts in confusion. Even the Roman centurion, one of the soldiers who had helped to crucify Jesus, recognized Him as being "the Son of God" (see Matthew 27:54; Mark 15:39).

For *fifty days* all that the people who had crowded into Jerusalem could see was an empty tomb. Pilate and the Jewish leaders knew that Jesus had been resurrected. No search party was sent. The apostles were not questioned. The enemies knew before the disciples did.

Jesus had been resurrected. He did not die again; rather, after appearing to His disciples over a period of forty days (Acts 1:3), He ascended to His Father in heaven. He was taken up in the clouds and is now seated at God's right hand (Ephesians 1:20; Colossians 3:1). Before He ascended, Jesus told His apostles, "But you will receive power when the Holy Spirit has come upon you; and you shall be My witnesses both in Jerusalem, and in all Judea and Samaria, and even to the remotest part of the earth" (Acts 1:8). This promise was fulfilled only days later, on the Day of Pentecost.

On that occasion God came with a mighty wind. The Holy Spirit filled the apostles. Divided tongues as of fire sat upon them. All of the apostles began to preach in other languages the wonderful things of God. Then, in the major sermon, Peter preached about what had happened *fifty days before*! He said his listeners were not only witnesses but also perpetrators. He branded them as murderers—killers of God's Son! They were cut to their hearts. They cried out in terror. They repented. Three thousand were baptized for the forgiveness of their sins. With their conversion, the church began on this Day of Pentecost in Jerusalem.

History reveals to us that "all the armies that ever marched, all the parliaments that ever sat, all the kings that ever reigned"[1] have not affected us as the one solitary life of Jesus Christ has. Those three thousand baptisms were no accident. Satan was not as smart as he thought he was. Do not underestimate Satan; do not overestimate Satan. Did Satan think he could kill God? Surely, he knew that, even if he did kill God, he could not keep God dead. Imagining that he had won, Satan defeated himself.

The cross . . .
there is no other way!

---

[1] James Allan Francis, "Arise, Sir Knight," in *"The Real Jesus" and Other Sermons* (Philadelphia: Judson Press, 1926), 123–24.

18

Things Connected with the Cross

Ephesians 5:21–32

". . . Christ also loved the church and gave Himself up for her, so that He might sanctify her, having cleansed her by the washing of water with the word" (Ephesians 5:25, 26).

God meets sinners only at the cross. However, the blessings of God are received on God's terms—not ours. We must plant the cross in the middle of our hearts, and then God plants us in the middle of His salvation.

The cross is central; things connected with it are paramount. If you spend money to buy a suit, the good from that money comes from wearing the suit. Medicine can heal, but only when you take it. Medicine left in bottles is worthless. Paul said, ". . . not in cleverness of speech, so that the cross of Christ would not be made void [or lose its power]" (1 Corinthians 1:17). The power is there, but we must be connected to it.

THE NEW TESTAMENT

Jesus said, "For this is My blood of the covenant [testament], which is poured out for many for forgiveness of sins" (Matthew 26:28). The Bible is a book about blood. The word "blood" is mentioned over four hundred times. Are we too proud to be associated with blood? Is it too messy? Had uninspired men written the Bible, they would have covered it with sunshine; God, the One who wrote it, stained it with blood.

Too many think the cross of Christ was defeat and His resurrection was victory. The New Testament only reveals His *death* as the victory. Hebrews 9:15, 16 pictures Jesus as the mediator of the new covenant, or testament. A testament (or will) is good only upon death. Jesus took the power of death from Satan through His death. The resurrection validates the death! Jesus won at the cross. Paul said, ". . . And He has taken it out of the way, having nailed it to the cross. When He had disarmed the rulers and authorities, He made a public display of them, having triumphed over them through Him" (Colossians 2:14, 15).

Jesus is the key to the Scriptures. You can find Jesus implied in every verse. The "Living Word" is only found in the "Written Word."

Let us be just Christians, *period*! The issue is authority: Will we go by the Bible or not? Let us just be members of Christ's church . . . no more, no less. Would you have liked to be a member of the first-century church? You can! God will add you to it, if you follow His Word.

THE NEW TESTAMENT CHURCH

The Gospels focus upon Jesus; Acts through Revelation focus upon His church. Jesus promised Peter that He would build His church (Matthew 16:13–20). He purchased the church with His own blood (Acts 20:28). He loved the church and gave Himself for it (Ephesians 5:22–30). Just as a husband ought to love his wife, Jesus loved the church and gave Himself that He might present to Himself a glorious church at the end of time (vv. 25–27).

The benefits of His blood come in, through, and by His church.

You cannot separate Christ from His church. The physical body of Christ purchased the spiritual body of Christ. The church is "God's forever family." Nothing on earth is like it. Nothing on earth can do what the local church does when it is doing right. All that Jesus left upon the earth was His church. He did not die for man-made organizations. Christ is head over all things to the church, which is His body (Ephesians 1:22, 23; Colossians 1:18). Unity and equality are only found in God's church. Jesus broke down the wall, reconciling both to God in one body through the cross (Ephesians 2:13–22). The church is one, not many.

You may say, "But the church cannot save you!" True! Christ is the Savior—the church is the saved. The saved were added to the church (Acts 2:41–47). If you are saved, you have been added; if you have been added, you are saved. God does not forget. *There are no saved people outside the church.* When you preach Christ, you get the church. The church is universal, but the only way to live as part of Christ's church is to be an active member of a local congregation of it. The local church is the only stable, secure place on earth.

Some say, "I'm against organized religion!" Then are they for "disorganized religion"? I have also heard, "I love Christ, but I reject the church." This is neither scriptural nor reasonable. The greatest joy of happily married men is their wives. They would rather hear a compliment about their wives than themselves. Some of them will not even verbally defend themselves—but they will not allow anyone to harm their wives or speak against them! Who would wish to stand before God having harmed Christ's church, His bride? At the end of time, Christ is going to present to Himself a glorious church not having "spot or wrinkle or any such thing" (Ephesians 5:27).

THE LORD'S DAY, THE LORD'S SUPPER

The Lord's Supper connects with the cross. The early church steadfastly assembled every Lord's Day, that is, Sunday (Acts 20:7; 1 Corinthians 16:1, 2; see Acts 2:42; Hebrews 10:25). The Lord's Supper was served in the assembly. The Christian does not partake alone and then assemble. The church that does not meet cannot survive. As a community, the church has a life of its own (Acts 2:42).

When the church assembles, Christ is present! Jesus is the host, not the guest! The Lord's Supper is not a church sacrament that forgives us—it is a memorial declaring that we are the forgiven. Jesus only has one command: "Follow Me." He only has one request: "Remember Me" (Luke 22:19, 20; 1 Corinthians 10:16; 11:23–26). He has one Bible, one bread, one cup, one body, one blood, and one covenant. Here is a good rule: The Lord's Supper every Lord's Day, and no Lord's Day without the Lord's Supper! Think what was used: the unleavened bread and the fruit of the vine. These emblems represent His body. It would be unthinkable to substitute anything for the bread and the cup.

The church does not grow on religious holidays, but it does grow on the Lord's Supper! To fail here is to make the church weak and sickly (1 Corinthians 11:23–30). The Lord's Supper is the greatest memorial on earth. Every member can participate. The focus is on the Word, the cross, and His forgiveness! Members examine themselves.

Members "proclaim the Lord's death until He comes" (1 Corinthians 11:26). This is why we take the Lord's Supper to those who are unable to leave their homes. They, too, are part of the body. The Lord's Supper is the one memorial around which the church rallies!

BAPTISM

The cross must be placed again at the center of society and not just on the steeple of a church building. Jesus was not crucified in a cathedral between two candles, but on a cross between two thieves. All of us must raise (and answer) the question "What must I do to be saved?" Some suggest "The Sinner's Prayer," based on Luke 18:9–14, when the tax collector prayed, "God, be merciful to me, the sinner!" To offer this as a way to salvation exposes our failure to study the Word or our failure to accept the Word, or both. In this story, both the Pharisee and the tax collector were Jewish brethren at the temple. Neither was a sinner who was coming to God for the first time. One was proud; the other was contrite. This is the lesson. This parable of Jesus was before the cross, the Book of Acts, the Great Commission, the Day of Pentecost, the preaching of the gospel, and the church. This incident was not about salvation. Jesus was not known, needed, or mentioned in this story!

Baptism connects sinners with the cross. Read Romans 6:3. In this act we contact the blood of Jesus; it is the only place on earth where a non-Christian can do that. Therefore, it must not be reduced to a meaningless church ritual.

The fact is that a non-baptized Christian is foreign to the Scriptures after Jesus went back to heaven. It is also foreign to the history of the first-century church. Baptism is an important event in salvation. Jesus put baptism in His Great Commission (Mark 16:15, 16). Sinners are baptized into the name of the Father, the Son, and the Holy Spirit (Matthew 28:18–20). The heart of the gospel message is the death, burial, and resurrection of Christ (1 Corinthians 15:1–4); sinners are baptized into His death, burial, and resurrection (Romans 6:3–6; Colossians 2:12). In baptism one accepts the Lord and is clothed with Him (Galatians 3:26–28). In scriptural baptism a sinner becomes a Christian (Acts 2:38).

Baptism is not a meritorious work of man, but the work of God. Each sinner must hear, believe, repent, and confess Jesus. No one can do these things for me, but someone else had to baptize me! Sinners, literally, "receive baptism." Twelve men were "rebaptized" by Paul in Ephesus because they had been baptized incorrectly (Acts 19:1–7). Paul believed that baptism was important and that it should be done properly.

Baptism saves (1 Peter 3:20, 21). The Jews on the Day of Pentecost needed to be baptized (Acts 2). The Ethiopian nobleman also needed to be baptized (Acts 8:26–40). Paul even needed to be baptized (Acts 9; 22:16). Cornelius, a Gentile (non-Jew), needed to be baptized (Acts 10). Who can read all these passages and not conclude that all accountable people need to be baptized?

THE CRUCIFIED LIFE

The cross results in the crucified life. Paul said, "I have been crucified with Christ; and it is no longer I who live, but Christ lives in me . . ." (Galatians 2:20, 21). Jesus lived the life before He died the death. Salvation is free, but it costs us everything—our lives! In the historical sense, Jesus is risen; but in the holy sense, He is still on the cross. The church was brought into existence through the cross and lives as an expression of the cross. We come to the cross and live at the cross, as Paul described in Colossians 3:1–4.

The crucified Savior can be communicated best by crucified servants. Jesus calls us to die. Paul died daily (1 Corinthians 15:31). The church can only learn how to live when it has the courage to die. The Christian must never be more like the world that Christ came to save than the Christ who died to save the world. All the Bible that one *really* has is what he lives. Give God the first fruits of your day, the first day of the week, the first portion of your pay, and the first place in your heart.

When you undermine the obedience of faith, the book of blood, the blood-bought church, the Lord's Supper of remembrance, or baptism, nothing remains to connect you with the cross.

The cross . . .
there is no other way!

19
The Incarnation

John 1:14–18

"And the Word became flesh, and dwelt among us . . ."
(John 1:14).

Our heads ache at the thought of the incarnation (that is, God becoming one of us)! Man wants to be God—that, we surely understand. What we cannot understand is that the sovereign, infinite, immutable, eternal God became man . . . as a helpless baby! Only God could think of this! Only He could do this! This amazing fact is expressed in the Gospel of John through two unforgettable sentences: "In the beginning was the Word, and the Word was with God, and the Word was God"; "And the Word became flesh, and dwelt among us" (John 1:1, 14a).

THE SON OF GOD
BECAME MAN!

Jesus is the *only* mediator between God and man (1 Timothy 2:5, 6). He is the living bread from heaven (John 6:48–58). On the holy mountain God said, "This is My beloved Son, with whom I am well-pleased; listen to Him!" (Matthew 17:5; see 2 Peter 1:17, 18). The incarnation is the "miracle of miracles."

The heavenly Son of an earthly mother,
The earthly Son of a heavenly Father,
So divine, not human,
So human, not divine.

Jesus Christ could not be invented. God wrapped the truth of salvation in Jesus and sent Him to walk among us! Jesus never rebuked anyone who called Him God or worshiped Him. We could say that the coming of Christ in bodily form, as a man, is the heart of the Scriptures. Jesus is the *Logos*—the Living Word of God, who became a man! We believe that Jesus is God, but we must also believe that God is the human Jesus!

Christianity is essentially historical. It is not "the myth among myths," an allegory without substance. The greatest of all truths is that Jesus became one of us, lived as our example, taught us the truth of God, and died for us to bring us to God.

THE VIRGIN BIRTH

The deity of Jesus is unavoidably connected with the virgin birth (Matthew 1:18–25). If both parents of Jesus had been human, then His blood would have been as worthless as ours. He could not have resurrected Himself or anyone else. Hugo McCord said, "Christianity without the virgin birth becomes a religion without salvation by the blood and without a resurrection. It is reduced simply to a social gospel for this life only."[1]

Man probably stumbles more over Christ's humanity than His deity. While human, Jesus did not merely go through the motions of being a man, as if performing in

---

[1]Hugo McCord, "Jesus: Our Eternal Savior," in "Jesus Christ, the Divine Son of God," *Truth for Today* (May 2000): 6.

a play on a stage. In the garden real sweat dropped like blood from His face (Luke 22:44). His favorite title for Himself was "Son of Man," which is found more than eighty times in the New Testament. The deity of Jesus is best demonstrated by His humanity.

Sometimes we greet good news with skepticism, yet bad news we swallow at once. We do not have to prove absolute truth. Absolute truth proves itself. God is not running to be elected God. He *is* God. That is truth. The prime needs of religion today are doctrine, theology, and truth!

JESUS IS LORD

This Christ who became Man also was made Lord! Paul wrote,

> For this reason also, God highly exalted Him, and bestowed on Him the name which is above every name, so that at the name of Jesus every knee will bow, of those who are in heaven and on earth and under the earth, and that every tongue will confess that Jesus Christ is Lord, to the glory of God the Father (Philippians 2:9–11).

This fact of His Lordship is so simple, yet so profound! Think of it: We pray to God, whom we cannot see, and expect to go to heaven on the virtue of His Son, whom we have not seen in the flesh. The way up is down; we empty ourselves to be full. We confess being wrong to be made right. The strongest are the weakest; the poorest, the richest. We die to live and give to get.

The middle cross at Calvary was not Christ's—it belonged to all of us. Dying was Jesus' reason for becoming man. The entire emphasis of John's Gospel Account is the eternal significance of Jesus. The power to live the Epistles is found in the story of the cross in the Gospels.

This truth expresses the "amazing grace" of God. In the incarnation Jesus eternally connected Himself with humanity. We were never God and never will be God! Jesus was *both* totally humbled and totally exalted. His exaltation did not destroy His humanity; rather, it glorified His humanity.

The cross . . .
there is no other way!

20

God's Holiness

1 Peter 1:15, 16; Revelation 15:3, 4

". . . 'Holy, Holy, Holy, is the LORD of hosts, the whole earth is full of His glory'" (Isaiah 6:3).

First Peter 1:15, 16 says, "But like the Holy One who called you, be holy yourselves also in all your behavior; because it is written, 'You shall be holy, for I am holy.'" In studying the cross, we face the transcendent holiness of God!

God is holy! We are not asked to be as holy as God is; this would be a burden no one could bear (Acts 15:10). God is thrice holy. He is "Holy, Holy, Holy" (Isaiah 6:3). He is not just "love, love, love" or "law, law, law." God is God, and that means that He is holy! We must revere holiness in order to accept or allow for wrath. We cannot appreciate or accept grace until we understand wrath. The question is not "How can a loving God send a sinner to hell?" but "How can a holy God *not* send a sinner to hell?"

Our first problem comes when we do not see God as He really is. We must not bring God down to be like us. We must lift ourselves up to be like God. Sentimental ideas about God result in foolish talk about God. God, today, is "in"; but the "in" God is not a holy God! People today seek to *feel* God while refusing to know God and obey God (John 17:3).

God, in one sense, does not have attributes. He cannot be sliced up like pie. He is *"holy"*! Idols are not holy and cannot be holy! God's name is "Holy" (Isaiah 57:15). We need to recognize the "otherness" of God! He does not conform to a standard—He *is* the ultimate standard. He is an absolute, infinite, incomprehensible fullness of purity who is incapable of being anyone other than who He is. The Spirit of God is the Spirit of truth.

We must live in awe, in wonder of God! His being is unitary. He is not parts working together, but simply *One*! God is never at cross-purposes with Himself. One attribute is not in conflict with another. He is not a "walking civil war."

God is love (1 John 4:8, 16), but love is not God. God defines love; love does not define God. Love cannot make sense apart from holiness. What holiness demands, love provides. If God is only equal to love, then the personality of God is simply the attribute of love. If all other attributes are eliminated except this one (love), then this one attribute becomes a substitute for God. Love is something characteristic of God, but it is not God.

Holiness is the unique characteristic of God that separates Him from His created beings and any alleged gods. This allows God both to withhold His love and to give His love. No wonder the word "holy" is in the Bible over six hundred times! Only a superior power can compel obedience. In all eternity past, nothing has entered God's Being, and nothing has been removed.

We are to be holy! Holiness must be the business of every human being! Why has holiness fallen upon hard times? Tragically, the human race has orphaned it. Personal holiness has become obsolete. We do not even promote holiness enough in regard to Jesus. When was the last time you heard about "The Holiness of Jesus"? Holiness is not the way to Christ; Christ is the way to holiness. The Christian is not ruined by living in the world, but by allowing the world to live in him. Holiness is not only what God gives me, but also it is what I manifest in the life that God has given me. Holiness is a position, a practice, and a process.

Holiness cannot be exchanged for cheap, false spirituality. Spirituality can be faked or bragged about; holiness cannot. Can a person be proud of humility? Ironically, those who have great virtues are usually unaware of having them. Humble people deny their humility!

Without holiness, we cannot see God (Hebrews 12:14). Our hearts are to be blameless in holiness before God (1 Thessalonians 3:12, 13). We are to perfect holiness in the fear of God (2 Corinthians 7:1) and to be partakers of His holiness (Hebrews 12:10).

The cross . . .
there is no other way!

21

The Appeal of the Cross

1 Corinthians 1:18; Galatians 6:14

"'And I, if I am lifted up from the earth, will draw all men to Myself'" (John 12:32).

Why is the cross so appealing to us?

It appeals to our understanding. Christianity came from an event in history. It cannot be reduced to an idea, a philosophy, or a statement. It is a Person (Jesus Christ). It is not only what God said, but also what God did.

By worldly standards the life of Christ was a failure. Rome and Jerusalem were unchanged by it. When Jesus ascended to heaven, He left only 120 devout disciples in Jerusalem (Acts 1:11–15). They were unknowns, penniless and without political power (Acts 4:13). However, when Peter and the other apostles preached on the Day of Pentecost, about three thousand people were baptized. Anyone who thinks about it will conclude that the greatest event of all time is Jesus' dying for us. The God who made us became one of us in the person of His Son. He walked on earth with us and took our sins upon His shoulders to the cross! Amazing grace!

Nothing on earth is as powerful as the cross of Christ. Culture tries to offer Christ without a cross. Humanism offers a cross without a Christ. One is religion without sacrifice; the other is sacrifice without religion. Both fail!

The cross appeals to our deepest emotions. Jesus' dying on the cross stirs our indignation; it also inflames our admiration. The meaning of it breaks our hearts. Jesus said, "And I, if I am lifted up from the earth, will draw all men to Myself" (John 12:32). The magnet of the cross draws people to God. The closer you get, the more powerful it is. You tremble; you cry; you rejoice! The cross can only be thought about and received with passion. Salvation is not a business transaction. Empathy, sympathy, anger, and joy are engendered within you! Every day there is something new, different, and poignant that arises from it.

The cross appeals to our human dignity. The all-powerful God could have coerced; instead, He invites. God does not bully. Jesus draws—not drives—people to God (John 6:44–47). The cross does not push, intimidate, or manipulate people. Paul called the earthly life and death of Jesus the "mystery of godliness" (1 Timothy 3:16). No "myth" can change a person. Jesus changes people. His love changes people. He loved us enough to give His life in our stead, so that we might live with Him eternally—but He lets us decide.

The cross appeals to our sense of moral obligation. The cross is God's "plus" sign for all that is "minus" from the world. No one can remain neutral at the foot of it. Scheming Caiaphas, cowardly Pilate, and heartless Herod have all been judged by history. Who won? Jesus Christ! He calls us to share in His victory and to call others to share in it with us. There is no end to the cross. It must be given to others; it is the only thing worth giving. Nothing we can do by ourselves has any worth to it in the long run! It is unthinkable that sinners could glory in anything else but the cross.

The story of the cross is the greatest story ever told. It has the truest, deepest, and purest appeal!

The cross . . .
there is no other way!

22

The Mystery of the Cross

Romans 16:25–27; Colossians 1:25–28; 2:2, 3

"By common confession, great is the mystery of godliness: He who was revealed in the flesh, was vindicated in the Spirit, seen by angels, proclaimed among the nations, believed on in the world, taken up in glory" (1 Timothy 3:16).

"Mystery" is not to be understood as "mysterious" (as is the case with mystical ecstasies, vibrations, the occult, or hobgoblins). Mystery and superstition have nothing in common. People love the magical, the bizarre, and the sensational. We are more interested in teasing our curiosity than understanding the truth. God gives us the right kind of mystery in the gospel message. The simple and divine things always have a mystery to them (such as marriage; Ephesians 5:20–33).

We can easily say more than we can understand. "Mystery" does not refer to something we need a detective to investigate. It is not the absence of meaning, but it is the presence of a greater meaning than we can comprehend. The fact that you cannot fully understand something does not mean that you cannot understand it at all. No one can fully grasp love, faith, justice, or goodness; but we believe in them and seek to exhibit them.

The cross is the greatest mystery of God. A little child

can drink of it; old men can meditate upon it for a lifetime. Still, people do not know even a "thimbleful" about it. It is "unexplainable," yet we can grasp the import of its eternal truth. Mystery challenges and allows growth. Creeds do not have mysteries.

A mystery defies our grasp and is difficult to communicate. Eternal principles are larger than human words. We think we know who we are, but we finally recognize that we are seeing ourselves through a darkened glass! (See 1 Corinthians 13:12.) We have daily surprises that result in our saying, "I never understood this!" Sinful man is always strong in things that do not matter but weak in eternal things that do matter. We do not conquer mystery—we use it, grow in it, and celebrate it.

Mystery is understood only by revelation, not by reason. God can be known but not figured out. We cannot understand God's grace until we accept His wrath. Until we understand the cross, we cannot understand Christianity.

Where there is no mystery, there is no wonder. Without wonder, there is no real worship. When one explains a magic trick, he finds nothing is left; when we accept God's mystery, we find everything!

Mysteries are not discovered in Eastern religion or Western logic. Mystery comes only by divine revelation. A mystery is an eternal secret that can be disclosed by God alone. A truth once hidden is now revealed. The secret things belong to God . . . but they are revealed to us. We do not have to be "one of the initiated" or know the "secret handshake" to enter the mystery of God.

Paul said that the gospel message is a mystery (Ephesians 6:19). Faith is a mystery (1 Timothy 3:9) to be lived in a pure conscience. Redemption in Christ is the mystery that saves and unites Jews and Gentiles (Ephesians 1:7–13). Paul said that this truth about Christ had been kept secret since the world began (Romans 16:25, 26; 1 Corinthians 2:7). This mystery was "for obedience to the faith" (Romans 1:5; NKJV). The mystery by revelation tells us what to believe and what to obey. The Spirit has revealed through His holy apostles and prophets this mystery of grace (Ephesians 3:2–6). This truth, this unity, had not been previously made known. Paul also referred to "Christ and the church" as a "great mystery" (Ephesians 5:32). He used this description in regard to husbands and wives and the depth of marriage (Ephesians 5:21–33). All the beautiful things, the great things in life, involve mystery.

One of the great revelations of truth is found in Ephesians 3:9–11. God created all things in and for Christ. God planted a cross in His mind and heart before the creation. Christ fulfilled His plan on the cross. His blood purchased the church (Acts 20:28). Now, the manifold wisdom of God is displayed only in Christ by His church. This is God's eternal purpose. Mystery requires obedience without full knowledge. We are simply to trust and obey the plain truths of the Scriptures and grow in the knowledge of the Word every day! We must know enough not to deny what we cannot understand.

Great living demands a great mystery! Our deepest passion must focus upon things too wonderful to be fully understood, such as "the mystery of Christ, which in other generations was not made known to the sons of men, as it has now been revealed to His holy apostles and prophets in the Spirit" (Ephesians 3:4b, 5).

The cross . . .
there is no other way!

23

God's Power and Wisdom

1 Corinthians 1:18—2:5

"But by His doing you are in Christ Jesus, who became to us wisdom from God, and righteousness and sanctification, and redemption" (1 Corinthians 1:30).

The Bible says, "Christ [is] the power of God and the wisdom of God" (1 Corinthians 1:24). This verse defines Jesus as Lord. God has put in Jesus everything that we need. We are complete in Him (Colossians 2:10). Christianity is Christ. The Christian's power is in God's Christ, not in man's method. The abundant life can only be built upon Jesus. Christianity is radical and demanding. Man does face-lifts and makeovers; God only does heart transplants. Christianity is a Person, not a program.

Sin drains the gospel's power out of our lives (1 Corinthians 1:17; NIV). Christianity makes a person a new creation and gives him a new life and mind (2 Corinthians 5:17; see John 3:1–7; Galatians 2:20). Jesus calls us to die to sin that we might live to God.

The cross turns our normal way of thinking upside down. It says that we die to live and we give to get. It says that the way up is down and the last shall be first.

A crucified God is an oxymoron. He is almighty, but He has allowed Himself to be human. A Christian also is an oxymoron. He is a living dead man. He has died, yet he is fully alive! People want life—but the cross offers death as the way to life. People crave victory—but the cross is a defeat that leads to victory. People want comfort—but the cross pricks our consciences and guides us to obey the gospel so that we may take comfort in God's forgiveness. People want peace—but the cross brings us to a war that results in peace. People honor beauty—but the cross, crude and ugly, expresses a beauty that excels all other beauties. If we wish for the power and wisdom of God, we begin with Christ upon a cross.

CHRIST, THE POWER OF GOD

Paul said that "the power of God for salvation" is in the gospel message (Romans 1:16). What kind of God would save sinners through a cross? A God of grace and forgiveness! Our world worships brute power. God's power is greater than all other powers combined. It is awesome, everlasting, and full of mercy.

God created and upholds the world by His Word (Genesis 1; 2; Hebrews 1:3). He has providential power, for He works out all things for good for those who love Him (Romans 8:28).

However, God's greatest strength is revealed in the cross. It is a power that is described as His weakness! Paul said that He "has chosen the weak things of the world to shame the things which are strong" (1 Corinthians 1:27).

He is a God of infinite humility. He provides salvation for us, but He lets us choose whether or not we will take it. He does not force His way into our lives—He stands at the door and knocks (Revelation 3:20). In the free choice that He gives us, we see the humility of God. He teaches in His approach to us that we cannot make anything grow by pounding it with a sledgehammer.

Nothing is more helpless than a naked man dying on a cross, but God's greatest work was done through a Man, His Son, on a cross. Consider the power of the cross: There is no sinner for whom Jesus did not die, and there is no sin the cross cannot take away.

Jesus' death at Calvary was not a freak experience. It was the fulfillment of an eternal truth that was announced before the world began. Jesus was not on the cross for merely six hours. In a sense, He was there for thirty-three years. He faced it every day of His earthly life.

Jesus is the source of our salvation; the cross was the means of our salvation. God's power is made perfect in weakness (2 Corinthians 12:6–10). Although crucified through weakness, Jesus exhibits the power of God (2 Corinthians 13:4). All we can do with it is to receive it humbly. If we reject it, we will do so to our eternal destruction.

The German philosopher and atheist Friedrich Nietzsche idolized power. He despised Jesus because he thought He was weak. Nietzsche is dead; the gospel is still being preached.

CHRIST, THE WISDOM OF GOD

Paul said that Jesus "became to us wisdom from God" (1 Corinthians 1:30). God's great power is guided by His wisdom. His great plan for our salvation is an expression of His great wisdom.

God, in His wisdom, put a cross at the center of Christianity. Man thinks the cross is grotesque, but God says that it is the fullness of His glory.

The sin that underlies all sin is presumption (Psalm

19:13; 2 Peter 2:10). Man presumes that the way he thinks is the way God thinks, or should think. Psychology promises to make life *better*. Christ gives sinners life, *period!* Dead men need life, not rehabilitation (Ephesians 2). The power of God has always been to raise the dead. At the cross God raises sinners from the dead.

Man wants salvation from war, poverty, and disease. Christ on the cross saves us from sin. Man cannot solve war, mistreatment of others, or social unrest until he is saved from sin. Sin can be cured only at the cross.

To the intellectually proud, the cross is still folly. Man wants power, not wisdom—enlightenment, not faith. One cannot hold to the cross and at the same time hold to pride, hatred, and sin. No one can stand at the cross and boast.

At the cross Jesus died to save a world that did not want to be saved. What a Savior! Paul determined to know nothing but Christ and Him crucified (1 Corinthians 2:1–5). Believe it and teach it! Never lose faith in the power of the gospel message! Let us quit trying to be godly without God, to be Christians without Christ, to be spiritual without the Spirit.

Only God could take an instrument of execution (the cross) and make it into the greatest motivation upon earth. Apart from the cross, there is no power to die to self, and there is no wisdom with which to live life to the fullest. Jesus said, "And I, if I am lifted up from the earth, will draw all men to Myself" (John 12:32). He was able to draw all men to Himself because the cross is invested with God's wisdom and power.

The cross . . .
there is no other way!

24

Prophecy

Matthew 26:56a; John 5:39

"'But the things which God announced beforehand by the mouth of all the prophets, that His Christ would suffer, He has thus fulfilled'" (Acts 3:18).

Those who do not want to believe have little interest in prophecy. *Think about it!* Prophecy is a powerful evidence to the integrity of the Bible. God kept every one of His promises. Floyd Hamilton noted that there are 332 fulfilled prophecies concerning Jesus in the Old Testament.[1] Some are very specific. No other religion has a prophesied founder and Savior!

It is not by chance that Jesus began His public ministry claiming to be the prophesied Messiah (Isaiah 61:1–3; Luke 4:16–27). The listeners did not misunderstand what He said. In anger they tried to kill Him (Luke 4:28–30). Men even tried to abort His ministry in His own hometown!

Consider the many prophecies Jesus fulfilled.[2] He was the seed of Abraham (Genesis 22:18; Acts 7:1–6; Romans

---

[1]Floyd Hamilton, *The Basis of Christian Faith*, rev. and enl. (New York: Harper and Row, 1964), 160.

[2]See Hugo McCord, "Jesus: The Fulfillment of Prophecy in His Life," in "Jesus Christ, the Divine Son of God," *Truth for Today* (May 2000): 9–17.

101

4:13–25; Galatians 3:6–16), a prophet like Moses (Deuteronomy 18:15–22; Acts 3:22–26), and the seed of David (John 7:42; Romans 1:3; 2 Timothy 2:8). He spoke in parables (Psalm 78:2; Matthew 13:34, 35). He was the son of a virgin (Isaiah 7:14; Matthew 1:23–25), a Galilean (Isaiah 9:1, 2; Mark 14:70; Luke 22:59), the light of the Gentiles (Isaiah 49:6; Acts 13:46, 47), a lowly king (Zechariah 9:9; Matthew 21:1–8), the Branch (Jeremiah 23:5; Hebrews 7:14), called out of Egypt (Hosea 11:1; Matthew 2:15), and a Nazarene (Matthew 2:23). He was declared to be our Savior before the foundation of the world (Ephesians 1:3, 4; 3:9–11; 1 Peter 1:20).

Some of these prophecies are given in generalities. However, especially in regard to the cross, there are several minute specifics: the manner of His death (Psalm 22:16; Zechariah 12:10; John 12:32), a public death (Deuteronomy 21:22, 23; Acts 5:30; 10:39; 13:29; Galatians 3:13; 1 Peter 2:24), betrayal by a friend for thirty pieces of silver (Psalm 41:9; Zechariah 11:12; Matthew 26:14, 15; 27:3–10), silence before His accusers (Psalm 38:13; Isaiah 53:7; Matthew 26:59–63; Mark 14:55–61; 1 Peter 2:23, 24), being with thieves (Isaiah 53:12; Matthew 27:38; Mark 15:28; Luke 23:39–43), and experiencing pierced hands and feet (Psalm 22:16; Zechariah 12:10; John 20:27). Lots were cast for His clothes (Psalm 22:18; Mark 15:24; John 19:23, 24), and none of His bones were broken (Psalm 34:20; John 19:36). He was offered gall and vinegar to drink (Psalm 69:21; Matthew 27:34; John 19:28–30), was forsaken by God (Psalm 22:1; Matthew 27:46), was buried with the rich (Isaiah 53:9; Matthew 27:57–60), and became the rejected cornerstone (Psalm 118:22, 23; Matthew 21:42; Acts 4:11; Romans 9:32, 33). On the Day of Pentecost, Peter declared that the lowly king who had come riding upon a donkey (Zechariah 9:9; Matthew 21:1–11) was "both Lord and Christ" (Acts 2:36).

Isaiah is called the "Messianic Prophet" because of His numerous prophecies concerning the Messiah. His writings are quoted more than fifty times in the New Testament.[3] Six hundred years before Christ, he was inspired by God to give a detailed picture of the Messiah. Isaiah 53 is the "Holy of Holies" in the Old Testament, the "Suffering Servant Song." The Jews wanted a political, military victory. The idea of a suffering, dead Savior never crossed their minds. Be merciful with them. It is difficult to imagine the God of heaven dying upon a cross!

Phrases from Isaiah 53 are repeated at least six times in the New Testament![4] Philip told the Ethiopian nobleman that the Man of Isaiah 53 was Jesus (Acts 8:30–35).

All the verbs in Isaiah 53 are in the past tense. The future was being declared as history. God (Jesus) is the same yesterday, today, and forever. With God the past, present, and future are all the same in reality. God's prophecies are so true that they could be recorded in the past tense. Jesus fulfilled all the prophecies made about Him. He prophesied His own death, burial, and resurrection and fulfilled these prophecies in detail.[5] The life and death of Christ are the most certified facts on earth!

The cross . . .
there is no other way!

---

[3]Gleason L. Archer and Gregory Chirichigno, *Old Testament Quotations in the New Testament* (Chicago: Moody Press, 1983), 92–134.

[4]Ibid., 120–24.

[5]See Matthew 16:21 (and Mark 8:31; Luke 9:22); 17:22, 23 (and Mark 9:30–32; Luke 9:43, 44); 20:17–19 (and Mark 10:32–34; Luke 18:31–33); Luke 24:7, 44–46; John 13:19.

25

The Problem of Sin

Romans 3:23; 6:23

"For all have sinned and fall short of the glory of God" (Romans 3:23).

How can someone want to be saved if he does not know he is lost? How can anyone say that sin does not exist?

A MAIN THEME

Sin is one of the main topics in the Bible. God gave the law of Moses to make people aware of sin: "Because by the works of the Law no flesh will be justified in His sight; for through the Law comes the knowledge of sin" (Romans 3:20). The Jew was right when he asked, "Who can forgive sins but God alone?" (Mark 2:7; Luke 5:21). With mankind, the problem of sin is insurmountable! Sin cannot be covered up; it can only be forgiven. When we understand what sin is, we are amazed—not at why God finds it difficult to forgive, but why He finds it necessary to do so at all! Can man in sin be saved? Can God, who is "holy" and far removed from sin, forgive sin? (Isaiah 6:3; see Revelation 4:8). He is transcendent holiness. Only through the cross can this righteous God pardon us.

COSMIC CONSEQUENCES

Adam and Eve took "just one bite of fruit." That is all it took! No murder, immorality, theft, abuse, or ill treatment was required to coerce mankind to sin. Everything changed in heaven, in hell, and on earth when Adam and Eve sinned! All was different with God, man, and Satan! Everything within man changed. He became alienated eternally from God and distanced from his mate. Mankind would never be the same. No wonder God said to Adam, "Where are you?" (Genesis 3:9). Read Genesis 2 and 3 and tremble! Man is a fallen, condemned sinner.

There is more to this history than "one bite." Adam and Eve allowed Satan to enter their lives. They listened to Satan, believed him, and obeyed him. They disobeyed God. God is God, and man belongs to Him by right of creation. Adam and Eve rebelled against God's authority.

A person can only be tempted when he is led away by his own lusts (James 1:14). He sins within before he sins without. Sin is the supreme choice of self. It is the refusal to let God be God; it is man trying to be more than man. Sin is our thinking that we know more, or know better, than God.

Man's relationship with God is now broken, betrayed, and destroyed. Sin matters to God. In reality, man, when he sins, decides to become his own god.

Away from God, sinners are dead in their sins (Ephesians 2). The wages of sin is death (Romans 6:23). Our sins, if not forgiven, eternally alienate us from God (Isaiah 59:2, 3). All the war, violence, and chaos in history began with that "one bite." God told Adam about this before it ever happened. However, God was displaced. Since then, Satan has been the god, prince, and father of this world (John 8:44; 12:31; 14:30; 16:11; 2 Corinthians 4:4).

To be saved, sinners must see sin as God sees it. Repentance will not come until sinners sense the horror of sin. People who do not fear God do not fear sin. People with a holy view of God sense the enormity of sin.

God hates sin, and we must hate it; but, sadly, too many do not hate sin as sin. The more holy we become, the more we hate sin because we understand what it does to our relationship with God.

HOPELESS AND HELPLESS

Man in sin cannot save himself. He cannot earn, buy, or deserve salvation. He cannot know enough or do enough to be saved. All that a sinner can do is repent and obey God. No one else can do that for him.

Jesus did not come to die for our hurts or habits. He died for our sins (Romans 5:6, 8; 1 Peter 1:18, 19). When we come to Him, we are washed in His blood (1 Corinthians 6:11; Hebrews 10:19; Revelation 1:5; 7:14). Jesus was made to be *sin,* but not a *sinner* (2 Corinthians 5:14–21).

The choice is ours. We can have our sins punished at the cross through Jesus or have the punishment fall upon us in hell for eternity.

We have only one way to deal with our sins: We must let Jesus forgive them. In order for Him to do this, we must repent of our sins, die to them, and have them washed away in baptism. (See Acts 2:38; 22:16; Romans 6:1–7; 1 Peter 2:24.)

The cross . . .
there is no other way!

26

Wrath

Romans 5:6–11

"Much more then, having now been justified by His blood, we shall be saved from the wrath of God through Him" (Romans 5:9).

The ultimate sin is to tell God how He ought to be. New interpretations now tell us that God does not have anger. "He has only anguish," some say. Not so! God is heartbroken over sin, to be sure, but He also possesses wrath. This is expressed in Hebrews 10:26–31 and 12:28, 29, and it is demonstrated throughout the entire Bible.

A holy God is a God of wrath. The word "wrath" appears 189 times in the Scriptures. The word "wrath" is used in the Bible even more than is "grace." People today may cringe at the word, but without wrath there would be no need for grace. To lessen judgment is to minimize sin. God has wrath, fierce wrath, great wrath, and a day of wrath. Love demands wrath, but wrath is appeased by love. Wrath and love go together. They must not be separated. Love restrains wrath but does not destroy it. God has made promises. Some are positive; some are negative. God keeps *both*!

Modern interpretations also maintain that Jesus had no temper, that Christianity condemns *all* anger. Read the

Gospel Accounts. Jesus had a righteous temper! As Jesus cleansed the temple, He was not laughing and singing devotional songs of happiness. God has a righteous indignation. Ask Adam and Eve, Noah, Sodom and Gomorrah, Babylon, and Ananias and Sapphira![1] Romans is about grace, but it is even more about God's wrath. (The word "wrath" appears twelve times in Romans.) Paul, an inspired advocate of grace, used the word "wrath" twenty-one times in his epistles. "Wrath" is used more often than any other word in relation to God's judicial anger concerning the guilt of sin.

WHY?

Why wrath? *Sin!* Wrath is severe, righteous anger. Can God be angry? The real question is "Why isn't God *more* angry than He is?" Why does God put up with us? If you were in His place, would you? Why are we still alive? Sin is what God hates (Psalm 119:104). Every time we sin, we do what God hates. Sin is enmity against God, a mutiny, an insult to God. God gave man an incredible universe. Man treats it with contempt. Satan called God a liar (Genesis 3:3–5), and Eve believed Satan. What God hates, we bring into our lives when we live in sin.

With man, anger is a passion; with God, it is a principle. To some degree we know what sin does to man; we have no clue what it has done to God. God is the "Chief-

---

[1] In His righteous wrath, God cast Adam and Eve out of the Garden of Eden after they sinned (Genesis 3:1–24). Noah and his family were the only survivors of the great flood God sent to destroy the sinful world (Genesis 6:11—7:23). Because of their grievous sins, God likewise destroyed the wicked cities of Sodom and Gomorrah (Genesis 18:20—19:25) and the idolatrous nation of Babylon (see Isaiah 21:9). In the New Testament, Ananias and Sapphira were struck dead for lying to God (Acts 5:1–10).

Sufferer" in the universe. Sin nailed Jesus to the cross. God had reason for severe, righteous anger! If God could allow Jesus to be crucified, imagine what He can do to vile sinners! Man has anger toward anyone and anything that threatens or destroys what He loves. God is infinitely greater in law, justice, wrath, holiness, mercy, and goodness than we are. The more we sin, the less we seem to know about it. Sin is against God (Psalm 51:4) and, in one sense, only against God.

However, "wrath" is not God's final word. "Forgiveness" is. The unpardonable sin is to refuse to be forgiven, for we may reach a point where we cannot repent.

REPENTANCE

God is "slow" to wrath (Proverbs 14:29; Nehemiah 9:17; James 1:19). However, every impenitent sinner and every sin will be punished. All that sinners can do is repent. Sin is radical. Repentance must be radical also. Guilt matters. By sinning, man casts out God. By repenting, man casts himself out. Sinners must be delivered from sin and self. Therefore, the gospel message first tells us of our sinfulness and then tells us of our salvation. Repentance is a difficult command to obey, but we must obey it.

All the preachers in the Bible continually discussed one topic: "repentance." John the Baptist wore out one sermon outline: "Repent or Else." Jesus began His ministry by saying, "Repent and believe in the gospel" (Mark 1:15b). Forgiveness is impossible without repentance. John told flawed churches to repent (Revelation 2; 3). Even God cannot save sinners until they let Him. The world is disoriented concerning repentance. Religious groups try to offer salvation without truth, knowledge, repentance, or obedience. Sinners are under the wrath of God. The world wants a Christianity that has low demands and no commands. Do not equate unmerited love with unconditional forgiveness.

Who wants to repent? "Repentance" (Gk.: *metanoia*) is a second mind, a new mind, or a changed mind. Beliefs must be changed before behavior is changed. Changed lives are the fruit of repentance (Matthew 3:8).

Repentance is a response of faith to grace (2 Corinthians 7:9, 10; Romans 2:4). The prodigal returned home seeking to become an employee. The father's love changed his heart and his life (Luke 15:17–24). Sinners must hate sin as God does. Christians are to live in faith and in repentance.

The cross . . .
there is no other way!

27

The Blood of Jesus

Ephesians 1:7–12

"In Him we have redemption through His blood . . ."
(Ephesians 1:7).

As we think specifically about the precious blood of
Jesus, a "holy hush" falls over our hearts because we know
that we are entering the "Holy of Holies" of the Scriptures.

The centerpiece of the Bible is the blood of Jesus!
Nevertheless, people today are horrified by the subject of
His blood. Some claim that Christianity needs new sym-
bols. Such a view impugns the intelligence and the character of God, for God chose the blood of His Son as the
means of our salvation! He made His Lamb the center of
all history (Revelation 13:8). The cross is the place where
we see how our sin hurt God the most; it also is the place
where we see how God loved us the most (John 3:16). The
theology of heaven is Christ-centered, cross-centered, and
blood-centered.

THE ENORMITY OF SIN

No book in all the Bible clashes more violently with
the modern mind than Leviticus. "How did this book get

into the Bible?" we wonder. In our reading of the Bible, we usually skip it. However, this is a most important biblical book. It is where God detailed the sacrificial system of the law of Moses. It is filled with priests, sacrifices, and blood! God, in that book of law, was teaching the exceeding sinfulness of sin (Romans 7:13). It implies that God and sin cannot mix.

Sin contradicts God! It cannot be overlooked. Every sin and every impenitent sinner will be punished. Sin cannot be excused even by a divine decree—the righteousness of God prevents it.

Sin's sting is the sting of death (1 Corinthians 15:56). Forgiveness of sin can only come from the shedding of blood. Under the Law, forgiveness of sin required the blood of animals (Hebrews 9:22). The Law is our teacher to bring us to Christ, the final and full offering for sin (Galatians 3:22–29; see Romans 15:4; 1 Corinthians 10:11).

The old sacrificial system of Moses, with its blood of bulls and goats, could not take away sin (Hebrews 10:4). In addition, man could not perfectly keep the Law (Acts 15:8–11), and not even the blood of mankind could atone for man's guilt. What man could not do for himself, God did for him. Robert Coleman counted 460 specific references to blood in the Scriptures.[1] No one who carefully reads the Scriptures can miss the fact that Jesus' shedding His blood for our redemption is at the center of Christianity. The testimony of the Holy Spirit is that Jesus' blood has created a "blood bank in heaven" that is always full. Paul said that Jesus died for our sins according to the Scriptures (1 Corinthians 15:1–4).

---

[1]Robert Coleman, "The Gospel of Blood" (http://www.preaching.com/preaching/pastissues/robertcoleman.htm; Internet; accessed 1 December 2006).

The perfect blood of Jesus reconciles us (2 Corinthians 5:14–21), washes us (Revelation 1:5; 7:14), redeems us (Ephesians 1:7; 1 Peter 1:18, 19), cleanses us (1 John 1:7), justifies us (Romans 5:8, 9), sanctifies us (Hebrews 10:10; 13:12), propitiates for us (1 John 2:2), gives us peace (Ephesians 2:13–16; Colossians 1:20), and enables us to overcome Satan (Revelation 12:11). The real, historical, full, and final payment for our sins is the blood of Christ. With John we say, "Behold, the Lamb of God who takes away the sin of the world!" (John 1:29, 36).

THE POWER OF HIS BLOOD

We see the power of His blood in its linkage with the New Testament (or new covenant; Matthew 26:26–28; 1 Corinthians 11:25, 26; Hebrews 13:20). Every word in the New Testament drips with the blood of Christ. When you read the Scriptures and fail to find Christ, you are misreading them. The blood of Abel cries out to God from the ground (Genesis 4:2–12; see Matthew 23:35; Luke 11:51). The blood of Jesus speaks of better things than does Abel's (Hebrews 12:24). "Listen" to the blood (Hebrews 9:11–22)!

We see His blood's power in its creation of the New Testament church (Acts 20:28; Ephesians 5:25–28). Millions of sacrificial animals and birds were offered under the law of Moses, but man was still mired in sin. Aren't you glad we are not under such a law system today? Animal blood could only buy some time, by rolling the sins forward for a year. The blood of Christ bought one glorious thing—the church!

The Old Testament says life is in the blood (Leviticus 17:11, 14). Jesus gave His blood to release us from our sins (Revelation 1:5). He died for us on the earth so that we might live with Him in eternity (1 Thessalonians 5:10).

The price of something grows out of its value. Jesus considered His church so valuable that He was willing to purchase it with His own blood (see Acts 20:28). The local church, with all its faults, is still the most powerful group on earth! To minimize the church is to denigrate the blood.

We see the power of His blood in the supper of the new covenant (Acts 2:42; 1 Corinthians 10:16–21; 11:24–30). There is one way, one body (the church), one bread, one blood, one supper, and one life! The blood is the fruit and the infinite power of the cross. The Lord's Supper proclaims Christ's death until He returns (1 Corinthians 11:26).

We see the power of the blood in the baptism of the Great Commission (Romans 6:1–5; Galatians 3:26, 27; Colossians 2:12). John said that three bear witness on earth—the Spirit, the water, and the blood (1 John 5:3–8). In baptism, sinners are clothed with the Christ of the cross. It is His blood that bestows upon us the right to enter heaven.

The world wants salvation without the blood, without the Bible, without the church, without the Lord's Supper, and without baptism. This is not God's plan! Our salvation comes through the blood of Jesus!

The cross . . .
there is no other way!

28

Big Words of the Cross, 1

Romans 5:11–21

"And not only so, but we also joy in God through our Lord Jesus Christ, by whom we have now received the atonement" (Romans 5:11; KJV).

"ATONEMENT"

Nothing in all of history is more amazing than the invitation of the Scriptures. God invites us to plumb the depths of the cross. When we do, we are stunned into silence and overwhelmed by gratitude.

Atonement, that is, being made one with God, is one of the great themes of the Bible. It is one truth that separates Christianity from all the other religions. One day in time— at the cross, in the death of Jesus—sinful man saw the eternal love of God (John 3:16).

Sin violates and eliminates holiness. Through sin, man separated himself from a holy God. No sinner has the right or the reason to stand in the presence of God. Can man in sin be saved? If so, how, when, and by whom? Sin is the greatest of all problems, but Jesus died to solve it.

Jesus did not come to seek the saved, but to seek the lost (Luke 19:10). Calvary is the incredible revelation that God is a pardoning God. Atonement is God's gift of love!

115

Atonement is beyond our comprehension and compensation. Faith believes that which can never be understood. It is better to accept a theology we cannot fully understand than to buy clarity at the price of inadequacy. There cannot be true fellowship with God without atonement. Jesus suffered the penalty that sin deserved. Therefore, sinners depend on the crucifixion. If sinners could have been saved another way, then God would have been a fiend to sacrifice His only Son. Jesus' accusers unknowingly spoke a profound truth: "He saved others; He cannot save Himself" (Mark 15:31; see Luke 23:35). Our Lord has no peers and no rivals. He is the Lion of Judah (Revelation 5:5), but He is also the Lamb of God. We identify more easily with the Lion. However, victory came not by the Lion, but by the Lamb (1 Peter 1:18, 19). The great teaching about the Lamb is in Revelation.[1]

The word "atonement" means "making amends, making things right, giving satisfaction to a wronged person." Atonement implies that "God is right." He is right about our problem—sin. He is right about the solution—the cross. Atonement is like a diamond: We cannot see all of it from any one direction. Cardinal errors result from emphasizing one facet of the cross over others. Jesus died on a cross—that is history. Jesus died for me—that is salvation. We must learn to believe and accept that Jesus died for each of us.

ATONEMENT AND JUSTIFICATION

It has been said that Romans is the heart of the Scriptures and Romans 3:20–26 is the heart of Romans. In this

---

[1]See Revelation 5:6, 12, 13; 6:16; 7:9, 10, 14; 12:11; 13:8; 14:1, 4; 21:9; 22:1, 3.

passage Paul used the phrase "... that He would be just and the justifier." Atonement is built upon justice. The Bible uses "justification" and "righteousness" in basically the same way. Obviously, one cannot teach justification without justice. How can God justify the guilty? Time and forgetfulness do not cancel sin. Sin cannot be fixed. Even God does not fix sin. The sin penalty must be paid, and sin must be punished. Jesus paid it all! Thus God's answer to sin is the cross.

Our culture stumbles over this truth (1 Corinthians 1:22–25). Man cannot see himself lost in sin. Universalism says, "God is too good to allow you to go to hell"—but "good enough" never is! A holy God cannot allow sin to remain unpunished. God is a God of justice. Do not accept the idea that "God is loving and will overlook sin"! Mercy cannot cheat justice. God cannot be less than what He is. Justice is a higher principle than sentimental love. What justice demanded, grace provided. What man could not do, God did in the Son of Man (Jesus).

Justice is the heart of biblical theology. Study justice! To believe in the cross is to accept justice and to accept hell. Love cannot make sense apart from justice (holiness). Without justice, grace is unnecessary. Without justice, the cross has no purpose. Love and holiness go together. If guilt does not matter, then Jesus died in vain. Sin must be cleansed—not overlooked (1 Corinthians 6:11).

The incarnation of Jesus, in and of itself, could not save us. The perfect life of Christ could not save us. The perfect teachings of Jesus, by themselves, could not save us. There had to be blood: "... [A]nd without shedding of blood there is no forgiveness" (Hebrews 9:22). There had to be death: "... since a death has taken place" (Hebrews 9:15–17; see 2:9; Romans 5:10; Colossians 1:22).

It was not love that nailed Jesus to the cross—it was love and justice. God is *just*. He also is the *justifier*. God is *right*. God provided by grace what man could not do by meritorious works. This is why Jesus cried out, "It is finished!" when He died upon the cross. "He paid a debt He did not owe; I owed a debt I could not pay."[2] Jesus could either save Himself or save us. He gave Himself to save us. The Judge of man became the Savior of man (John 5:22–27).

Therefore, salvation begins and ends with justification. In Christ, we have been justified. We have sinned, but God has forgiven us. The justice of God is so contrary to us that it even takes Christians by surprise!

ATONEMENT AND SUBSTITUTION

The middle cross at Calvary did not belong to Jesus; it belonged to you and me! His crucifixion was *vicarious, representative,* and *substitutionary*! Christ took a death that belongs to us; and when we come to Him and live in Him, we take a forgiveness He provided. Without substitution, the cross is only a story about a brave man who died a terrible death. Since we cannot save ourselves, someone else must save us if we are going to be saved.

What did I contribute to my salvation? My sin! Jesus is the perfect substitute in everything we were meant to be. The Son of God became the Son of Man, so that the sons of men might become sons of God. Christ's blood was first given *for* us, and then, daily it is given *to* us.

Can a person benefit from another's suffering and sacrifice? Yes! Life itself is filled with the concept of sub-

---

[2]Author unknown, "He Paid a Debt," *Songs of Faith and Praise*, comp. and ed. Alton H. Howard (West Monroe, La.: Howard Publishing Co., 1994).

stitution. It is logical, lawful, and expedient. The sacrificial system of the Old Testament teaches us this profound truth. The "scapegoat" is the vivid example. Beautiful Isaiah 53 reveals the depth of substitution. The heart of that text is sacrifice. Jesus is the Lamb slain from the foundation of the world (Revelation 13:8). Throughout its pages, the Bible affirms substitution.[3] Jesus was made to be sin. He became sin for us. Never was there more injustice and justice than at the cross!

How can the unrighteous be made righteous? Our righteousness is a "declared righteousness" (see Romans 3:25, 26; KJV; Philippians 3:9; James 2:23). No one can declare himself righteous (Romans 3:9, 10, 20). Self-justification is impossible. It is God who justifies (Romans 8:33), and He does this freely (Romans 3:24). This is a gift. A gift must have *both* a giver and a receiver. A gift is not a gift until it is received. Further, a gift is not a gift until it is used. We have a sin problem. Jesus, as our substitute, is the only One who can provide righteousness for us.

God cannot overlook or dismiss sin. He took our sin upon Himself and sentenced Himself for it. God's holiness was honored, our sin was punished, and those of us who have obeyed Him have been redeemed. God has declared the saved to be righteous. This is a legal (lawful) declaration. It is "justified justification."

In this process God is not making bad people good or evil people holy. Christians are faithful—not perfect. We are tempted and sinful; we fall short (Romans 3:9–12). Christians still live on the earth, in time, and in the flesh.

---

[3]See Romans 5:5–10; Ephesians 1:3–13; Philippians 3:7–10; Hebrews 2:9, 14–17; 7:25; 9:28; 10:10; 12:1, 2; 1 Peter 2:24; 1 John 2:1, 2.

Paul said that nothing good dwells in the flesh (Romans 7:18). Christians are at war . . . with Satan, sin, and self. However, Christians who are walking in the Light are constantly cleansed through His blood (1 John 1:7). God pronounces Christians legally righteous, free from any liability to the broken law, because He Himself, in His Son, bore the penalty. We were baptized into Christ and put on Christ in this act (Romans 6:3, 4; Galatians 3:26, 27). To be "declared righteous" changes not only our status, but also, gradually, changes our character and our conduct.

There cannot be justification without atonement. Obedient faith receives what grace freely offers. The cross is God's impenetrable mystery, a love greater than our minds can fathom. God is not, in reality, Someone we can understand, but He is Someone we can trust.

Critics of Christianity abhor substitution because substitution magnifies sacrifice. However, the entire concept of biblical religion is based on sacrifice. From Genesis to Revelation, God ordained that a sacrifice be made for sin. Jesus cannot be reduced to a good teacher, a benefactor, or a mere person—He is our sacrifice. God is both the reconciler and the reconciled. Jesus is humanity's substitute. He did not offer an animal; He offered Himself. The Book of Hebrews reveals Jesus as the unique priest and sacrifice. One writer said, "Christ saves us as a priest, by offering Himself as a sacrifice for our sins."[4] In the Old Testament, God had to see the blood on the doorpost in order to save each family as Israel was preparing to leave Egypt (Exodus 12:13). Everyone rescued by God has

---

[4]Charles Hodge, *Systematic Theology*, vol. 2 (New York: Scribner, Armstrong, and Co., 1876), 555.

thereby been purchased for God. Our bodies belong to God three times over—by creation, by redemption, and by the indwelling of the Holy Spirit.[5]

ATONEMENT AND ADOPTION

Nothing in our ministries is as exciting as helping parents to adopt a child. As the adoption papers are signed, we all think, "This child does not grasp how blessed he is." The concept of adoption is a neglected facet of Christianity. We seldom talk about or study the subject.

Let us change that and think about the Holy Spirit and His part in our adoption. To begin with, remember that we are born again of water and the Spirit when we become Christians (John 3:3–7). Being led by the Spirit, we become sons of God. He is the Spirit of adoption. He bears witness with our spirit (Romans 8:14–18). This makes us "fellow heirs with Christ." God wants sons, not slaves. God, who remained at a distance in the Old Testament, is to the Christian "Abba! Father!" This truth is beyond our understanding! Redemption makes adoption possible. The child of God is promised that the Holy Spirit cries, "Abba! Father!" in his heart (Galatians 4:4–7).

Amazing grace! By grace God predestined us for adoption by Jesus. God has accepted us in the Beloved, that is, in Jesus. Redemption comes through His blood. Upon obeying the gospel message of salvation, we were sealed with the Holy Spirit of promise (Ephesians 1:3–14). This is a "crown jewel" verse in the Scriptures. Here is the basis of our faith. John revealed the grand love of God—that forgiven sinners could be called the sons of

[5]God's way of living in the Christian's heart (see 1 Romans 8:9–11; 1 Corinthians 6:19, 20).

God. "Now we are sons!" John said (1 John 3:1, 2). What a profound thought! What a privilege! In this we see the Roman concept of freedom and sonship. Free! Restored! Adopted! Thank God! To claim Christ is to claim acquittal. We are incapable of winning the battle of life alone. God does what we cannot do, so we can be what we dare not think that we can be.

The cross . . .
there is no other way!

29

Big Words of the Cross, 2

2 Corinthians 5:17–21

"... God was in Christ reconciling the world to Himself, not counting their trespasses against them, and He has committed to us the word of reconciliation" (2 Corinthians 5:19).

"RECONCILIATION"

Salvation was and is by substitution. The object of substitution is reconciliation. Let us clear our minds of all prejudice and pre-conceived ideas regarding reconciliation, so that we can start at the beginning as we walk through the process of it. Because of its importance, let us make sure that we get this right.

Forgiveness is "in" today. Children are taught to say "I'm sorry" without thought, depth, repentance, or regret. Apology is "in"; confession of responsibility is "out." The Scriptures teach profound repentance. The word "apologize" is not even found in the Scriptures.

Picture two people who are close friends, and then the relationship is torn apart. For them to reconcile, their relationship has to be restored to the way it was. With reconciliation the lost is found, the dead is made alive, and the sin is forgiven. How can this be? First, the offended must want this restoration more than anything else. Second, the offender must want this restoration more than anything else. Society, today, just wants to be free from responsibility. *Both* the offended and the offender must be willing to pay any price for restoration. We must grasp this truth!

Forgiveness does not mean ending an argument yet living apart. Reconciliation is not a "Cold War." Too many sinners want forgiveness without reconciliation. They wish to be free from responsibility but not to be restored. To be forgiven means that we can be reconciled and can get along together again.

In one sense, the offender is at the mercy of the offended. Our text tells us that God reconciled us to Himself in Christ. God reconciled the world to Himself; God did not reconcile Himself to the world. Who moved first? God did! Jesus died for me before I repented! God provided forgiveness for me (through the gospel) before I was born! God wants sinners back! However, sinners must want to be taken back. Man is eternally lost unless God acts. We are His enemies, but we can be reconciled! Who moved first? Love responded first!

- Forgiveness is impossible without the grace of the offended.
- Forgiveness is impossible without the repentance of the offender.

It only takes *one* to forgive. It takes *two* to reconcile. We cannot help a man who will not help himself. Forgiveness is an unnatural act. The offended does not wish to pay the price; the offender does not want to repent. Nevertheless, they must do *both* to reconcile. Unless forgiveness leads to reconciliation, forgiveness fails.

Forgiveness is not the end (as our society thinks); rather, forgiveness is the means, and reconciliation is the end. Forgiveness does not merely free us from penalty; forgiveness allows us to restore a broken relationship.

THE LAWS OF "FORGIVENESS"

Shakespeare said, "To be, or not to be, that is the question."[1] Scripture says, "To forgive, or not to forgive—that is the issue." I must forgive. I must be forgiven. These are the big issues of life. Forgiveness is the bridge over which all must walk. What do we do when we forgive? What do we do when we accept forgiveness? Paul said, "Be kind to one another, tenderhearted, forgiving each other, just as God in Christ also has forgiven you" (Ephesians 4:32). Forgiveness begins with kindness. Be kind first! Then practice the laws of forgiveness. What are they?

The first law: The unforgiving cannot be forgiven. Read Jesus' prayer in Matthew 6:12–15; Mark 11:24–26; and Luke 11:4. (See also Matthew 18:35; Luke 6:37; 2 Corinthians 2:7.) Do not just learn the theory—start the practice! Our paramount purpose must be to learn to forgive. Be the first to forgive!

The second law: The offended must forgive, if only for sanity's sake! Without forgiveness, one can become bitter, mean, and angry. The past must not rule the future. Without forgiveness, one lives in chains. If you wait until the offender repents, you may waste your life waiting. Once you forgive in your heart, the offense ceases to be a primary issue—whether or not the offender repents.

The third law: There cannot be forgiveness without repentance. The chair and the plate belonging to the

[1]William Shakespeare *Hamlet* 3.1.56.

125

prodigal son were there even when he was in the far country (Luke 15), but he had to repent and return to use them. The prodigal left home to sin; to be forgiven, he had to stop sinning and return home (Luke 15:11–24). You cannot have forgiveness while living in the far country and sinning. The forgiveness was there—the unmerited yet conditional forgiveness of God. The father could not force the prodigal to return. God cannot save us until we let Him.

The innocent do not need forgiveness; they need to be defended and vindicated. Sinners are not innocent. Sinners are not victims. We must accept full responsibility for our sin. We must acknowledge guilt: "I did it." Read Psalm 51. Then we must repent (change). Someone may say, "It doesn't matter." Sin, offense, and betrayal matter! Sinners are violators!

Sin must be dealt with. Remember Peter? He was willing to forgive seven times (Matthew 18:21–35). Jesus multiplied that seventy times! He Himself used the number "seven" in Luke 17:3, 4. Peter was listening; but he was not thinking, learning, or beginning to practice. Nothing is too big or too much to forgive (Matthew 18:21–35). At the same time, forgiveness is not license to sin (Galatians 6:7).

Reconciliation is more than forgiveness. To reduce salvation to forgiveness is to rob it of its fullness. Repentance is not just turning from sin; it also involves turning to God. The prodigal could have been forgiven yet made a slave. God wants sons, not slaves (Luke 15). Sinners cannot accomplish their reconciliation, but they can reject it when God offers it. The popular attitude "I am not here to judge you" must be revised! Repentance involves judgment of sin. We will not engage in judgment, repentance, and forgiveness until we see sin the way God does. Repentance can never be too soon, but it can be too late.

The fourth law: Forgiveness does not guarantee a painless future. Forgiven sin still has consequences. Time and forgetfulness are not forgiveness. God remembers our sins no more (Jeremiah 31:34; Hebrews 8:12; 10:17), but this is not "spiritual amnesia." Sin has consequences. King David's baby died. Forgiven Israel was punished. Jerusalem was "wiped out like a dish" (in A.D. 70). Sinners still have nightmares. "My sin is ever before me," David wrote (Psalm 51:3b).

Forgiveness is a gift, yet it is the most costly thing on earth (Romans 5:10). Gifts like forgiveness are to be humbly received and greatly enjoyed. Only when we accept our forgiveness do we love as we can and should (Luke 7:36–50). Forgiving is not forgetting; it is starting all over again.

The cross . . .
there is no other way!

30

Big Words of the Cross, 3

1 John 2:1, 2

"And He Himself is the propitiation for our sins . . ."
(1 John 2:2).

"PROPITIATION"

The big word "propitiation" is one we have a hard time spelling and often mispronounce. This word presents a difficult concept because heathen practices have tarnished the concept. Pagan idols were portrayed as having childish whims that had to be appeased. In Jesus' time "propitiation" referred to appeasing the anger of an idol by making a blood sacrifice.

God does not have moods; He is above having hurt feelings. He created a salvation by which He could forgive mankind and remain just in His dealings with sin. Jesus provided this propitiation through His personal sacrifice. In a sense, God bore our punishment! In this way, He can be just and still save sinners.

Man must be righteous, but he cannot create righteousness because of his sinfulness. It is of God, but God cannot "just confer it" on sinners. Neither can sinners pay back, bribe, or impress God with lavish gifts. Jesus became the final, perfect sacrifice for us. He took upon Himself first our flesh, then our sin. He is *both* our sacrifice and our High Priest (Hebrews 2:14–18). He is *both* our Lord and our Savior (Acts 2:36). He is our vicarious sacrifice—the fulfillment of all Jewish sacrifices. He was not made guilty; He was made to be sin as our substitute for our sin (2 Corinthians 5:17–21).

Propitiation enforces the enormity of sin. Love without wrath is sentimentality. Divine grace satisfied divine wrath by a divine self-sacrifice.

"EXPIATION"

The New Testament says it is impossible for sinners to save themselves. Only Christianity has the Savior, Jesus.

Propitiation (with reconciliation as a result) is made possible by expiation (the act of making atonement). Propitiation and expiation are so intertwined that it is difficult to separate them. You expiate a sin, but you propitiate a person. Expiation is a doctrinal truth; propitiation is a personal application of a doctrinal truth. Expiation is the removal of guilt; propitiation is the removal of the divine wrath that has come because of the sin.

Jesus is our "mercy seat" (Romans 3:25, 26). Our righteousness is a faith-righteousness that comes through Christ. The blood of Jesus is our expiatory sacrifice. The cross is where the sin of man is judged. To expiate is to pay the penalty, the price (1 John 2:1, 2); to propitiate is to satisfy the justice of God. We were bought with a price, and a righteous God has declared us righteous through our faith in Jesus. We are declared forgiven because Jesus paid the price for our sin (see Hebrews 2:17, 18; 1 John 4:9–11).

Jesus is our "Passover" (1 Corinthians 5:7). He covered our sins, allowing God to put them behind His back (see Isaiah 38:17).

God did not stand apart from the cross in petulant anger. He involved Himself in our plight. In Christ, He took the penalty of our sins upon Himself—not in mechanical substitution, but in profoundly personal love. God cannot and will not forgive and accept us except through the cross.

"IMPUTATION"

The idea of imputed righteousness is profound yet simple. Sinful man cannot be righteous; therefore, imputed righteousness is the only kind of righteousness he can have. Justification has been called "the supreme paradox of the gospel." Through forgiveness, God makes sinners just, or righteous (Romans 8:1, 2).

Imputation is an accounting term which refers to another's riches being placed into my account. Our sins are imputed to Christ, and, as Paul said, we receive "the righteousness which comes from God on the basis of faith" (Philippians 3:9; see Isaiah 53:5, 6, 10, 11; Romans 4:11; 14:9; 1 Peter 2:24). Read and reread Philippians 3:7–11. We would prefer to merit grace, but grace cannot be merited! Burton Coffman well said, "Nothing that man could ever do in a million years of righteous living could ever earn the tiniest fraction of the salvation God gives to men in Christ."[1] Furthermore, imputed righteousness eliminates human pride. The only meritorious work in salvation is the cross.

"RANSOM"

The best-known and most misunderstood facet of atonement is "ransom." A ransom is the purchase price

---

[1]James Burton Coffman, *Commentary on Romans* (Austin, Tex.: Firm Foundation Publishing House, 1973), 122.

for freeing slaves, and sinners are the slaves of sin. God forever silenced Satan at the cross (Matthew 20:28; Galatians 3:13; 1 Timothy 2:5, 6; Titus 2:14, 15), where the blood of the Lamb was given to redeem us. What Satan thought was his greatest victory was his final defeat! Jesus died for us—as a price for our sin and a substitute for our death. He did not die as a martyr for a cause, but He freely gave His life as a ransom for us. Jesus made sin forgivable and man savable. Hallelujah, our Redeemer lives!

To whom was this ransom paid? God did not buy sinners back from Satan. God does not negotiate with anyone! We are "sold under sin" (Romans 7:14; NKJV), but we are not sold to Satan. God, not Satan, was satisfied at the cross (1 John 2:1, 2). Satan is the "accuser" (Revelation 12:9, 10). God cannot be holy without punishing sin. The penalty for sin had to be paid.

Neither was the ransom paid to society. Society has no law or court to deal with sin. The ransom was paid in order to satisfy the justice and holiness of God. Upon being ransomed, the debtor is totally owned. A ransom is satisfaction for the insult of sin. The penalty of law (Romans 6:23) is paid, and its sanctity is vindicated. The ransom reveals the seriousness of sin. Salvation is given to us as a gift when we believe and obey the gospel. Jesus not only dethroned Satan, but He also dealt with sin. In overcoming sin, Jesus overcame death. The sin-debt is unpayable except through the marvel of His grace.

The redeemed must not forget what redemption is!

The cross . . .
there is no other way!

131

31

Sanctified by the Cross

1 Corinthians 1:26–31

"But now having been freed from sin and enslaved to God, you derive your benefit, resulting in sanctification, and the outcome, eternal life" (Romans 6:22).

Christians exist to save sinners and make disciples (Matthew 28:18–20). However, evangelism, once "in," is now "out." "Why try to save someone who does not view himself as lost?" some now say.

DEDICATION
Sanctification has never been "in." Most of us do not even know what it is. "Sanctification," simply, is being "set aside, dedicated" for God's use. In religion, it means "holy." As Peter said, ". . . it is written, 'you shall be holy, for I am holy'" (1 Peter 1:15, 16). We can be right without being righteous (Matthew 6:1–18), but we cannot be righteous without being right. Sinners must be saved, and the saved must be sanctified.

Christians have been saved (that is salvation). Christians are being saved (that is sanctification). Christians will be saved (that is glorification). The saved need to be sanctified, not re-saved. God does not sanctify the unsaved.

We have salvation because of the position we have in Christ. Sanctification, however, is a process. Salvation comes through the event of our obedience to God; sanctification takes a lifetime. Paul wrote, "But we all, with unveiled face, beholding as in a mirror the glory of the Lord, are being transformed into the same image from glory to glory, just as by the Spirit of the Lord" (2 Corinthians 3:18; NKJV).

Let us not confuse salvation, sanctification, and glorification. We must learn to think in concepts. Most religious confusion comes from mixing up these three truths. Salvation is not an initial spasm followed by chronic inertia.

FAITH, NOT PERFECTION

Can one be a Christian without being perfect? Yes, for no Christian is perfect. People say, "I tried and failed, so I quit." Extremes come from misunderstanding concepts. "Once saved, always saved" is wrong. "Once saved, never saved" is equally wrong! Christians must know they are saved (1 John 5:11–13). We cannot be perfect; therefore, we must be saved by faith. We cannot be perfect, but we can be faithful one day at a time (Romans 3:10, 23). Faith works through love! (See Hebrews 11.) We cannot save ourselves by ourselves, so we must trust Jesus to save us. Our faith does not save us; the object of our faith (Jesus) saves us.

DAILY WALKING IN THE LIGHT

Saints sin even when we are walking in the Light. Read 1 John 1:7—2:3. The blood of Christ has saved us; His "blood of the covenant" also sanctifies us (see Hebrews 10:29b). Saints are constantly washed from sin and continually grow in sanctification.

Moses was given a law system; saints now live in a faith system. The most practical thing on earth is faith. We walk by faith (not perfection; 2 Corinthians 5:7). "The righteous man shall live by faith" (see Habakkuk 2:4; Romans 1:17b; Galatians 3:11b; Hebrews 10:38a). Let us pause and take special notice in the Scriptures when God quotes Himself!

The troubled "church of God at Corinth" was sanctified (1 Corinthians 1:2). As vile sinners, they had repented and their sins had been washed away (1 Corinthians 6:9–11). They had immediately become "saints" and then had begun growing daily in sanctification.

God (John 10:36; 1 Thessalonians 5:23) and Christ (1 Corinthians 1:30; Hebrews 2:11) sanctify. Christ's divine sacrifice, made once for all time, is the foundation of sanctification (Hebrews 10:10, 14, 16–24, 29; see Hebrews 7—9). Truth (John 17:17, 19), "the word of God and prayer" (1 Timothy 4:5), and the Holy Spirit (Romans 15:16; 1 Peter 1:2) sanctify. In addition to all of this, faith sanctifies (Acts 26:18).

What is the conclusion? Jesus did not save the Corinthians to leave them as they were. Saints must live in repentance. Children of God are "saints," even if they are not "perfect angels." A Christian grows in sanctification.

DISCIPLESHIP

Sanctification is discipleship, the process of learning and growing to be more like Christ. We are to have the mind of Christ (Philippians 2:5–11), daily buffet our bodies (1 Corinthians 9:23–27), and put off the old and put on the new (2 Corinthians 5:17; Ephesians 4:22–24). We grow in the grace and knowledge of Jesus (2 Peter 3:18). Through our growth, Jesus is being formed in us (Galatians 4:19). Every thought becomes captive to Him (2 Corinthians 10:5).

There are no spiritual hermits. God makes His church out of saints. No one can become a "spiritual giant" alone. We "stimulate each other to love and good deeds" (Hebrews 10:24). We are all part of the body. There are no "Lone Ranger" Christians. We do not withdraw—we serve as His body. We deny ourselves and take up our crosses daily (Luke 9:23–26).

The twentieth-century theologian Reinhold Niebuhr wrote:

> Nothing that is worth doing can be achieved in our lifetime; therefore we must be saved by hope. Nothing... makes complete sense in any immediate context of history; therefore we must be saved by faith. Nothing we do, however virtuous, can be accomplished alone; therefore we are saved by love.[1]

The cross...
there is no other way!

---

[1]Reinhold Niebuhr, *The Irony of American History* (New York: Charles Scribner's Sons, 1952), 63.

32

The Offense of the Cross

Matthew 16:16–23; 26:31–35;

Mark 8:27–33; 14:27–31

"But we preach Christ crucified, to Jews a stumbling block and to Gentiles foolishness, but to those who are the called, both Jews and Greeks, Christ the power of God and the wisdom of God" (1 Corinthians 1:23, 24).

The great apostle Paul said, *"God forbid that I should glory, save in the cross of our Lord Jesus Christ"* (Galatians 6:14a; KJV; emphasis mine). The glory of the cross comes out of the agony of the cross. The Son of God turned His death on the cross into a glorious victory.

God's great heart for people was revealed at the cross. He said it all through His Son's death. What more could He say? Satan has tried his hardest to blind us to the glory of the cross. He has sought to make it repulsive and ridiculous to our intelligence so that we will reject it. To recognize the "offense of the cross," therefore, is crucial. God has chosen to save us through the cross, but the devil seeks to lead us to scoff at it. If we do not understand the "offense of the cross," then we will probably miss what the god of this world, the devil, is doing! To misunderstand his designs is to allow ourselves to be deceived by them!

Sermons, songs, books, art, and daily conversations all vibrate with the cross. How, then, can there be any offense in it? Some talk of "sweet baby Jesus" or "a helpless man dying on a cross" and view Jesus as "a harmless man." This has made the story of the cross seem like a sentimental fairy tale. Popular preaching has removed the violence, blood, and cruelty inherent in the cross; it has made the cross painless and consequently sterile.

Probably no one living today has seen a crucifixion. Such a death was humiliating beyond words. From our setting, it is almost impossible for us to grasp the agony of it. We put the cross in our church architecture; we think of it as beautiful and ornate. However, the cross is not just "appropriate architecture"; it is not just "a meaningful story." Men glorify the cross while they miss the meaning of Jesus' death. The cross is not sentimental storytelling; it is the historic death of the Son of God for man's sins.

We love life; the cross is a presentation of death. We crave victory; the cross begins with defeat. We seek peace; the cross results from war. We love beauty; the cross is ugly. The cross is diametrically different from what mankind seeks to have. Critics protest, "How dare God be God!" Nevertheless, He is, was, and always will be! He, as the only righteous God, chose for His Son to bear our sins through an agonizing death on a cross.

Jesus sternly told His disciples that He would bring offense (Matthew 16:16–23; 26:31–35; Mark 8:27–33). Christ even used a Greek word that means "scandalized,"[1] saying that His followers would be offended in Him (Mark 14:27–31; John 6:60, 61).

---

[1] The Greek word for "scandalized," *skandalizo*, means "to fall away."

People *were* offended by Jesus and His death on the cross! They could not see how a crucified common criminal could be their Savior. In polite Roman society, the word "cross" was almost an obscenity, a word that was shunned in public. The thought of Jesus' being crucified was too much for Peter; he tried to protect Jesus from it. He was agitated. We do not want God to handle matters His way! Peter knew the Old Testament Scripture that pictured the tree (the cross) as a curse (Deuteronomy 21:23; Acts 5:30; see Galatians 3:13); he did not want Jesus to suffer such a death.

Jesus reacted quickly and firmly to Peter, identifying him with Satan (Matthew 16:23). People can rebuke their enemies, but they do not know how to rebuke their friends. Jesus reprimanded him and told him to get out of His way, for He was going to the cross.

The cross was the battleground for Jesus. He "sweated blood" in Gethsemane and prayed that God, if it were possible, would find another way (Luke 22:40–44). There was no other way but the cross.

Paul was not ashamed of the gospel (Romans 1:16, 17). Are we? The temptation is always to change the cross, to minimize it. Paul not only talked about "the offense of the cross" in Galatians 5:11 (NKJV), but he also revealed Christ as "a rock of offense" (Romans 9:31–33). He taught the cross as a stumbling block for the Jews and foolishness to the Gentiles (1 Corinthians 1:17–25).

We will not understand the salvation that Jesus brought until we understand the cross. At the cross God said that the only way to defeat sin is through the righteous judgment of sin. If the cross does not matter, then nothing matters!

Probably nothing on earth is as controversial, offensive, or divisive as the cross. No one ever made people angrier than Jesus did and does!

The cross offends because God, not man, is right. (1) God is right because our problem is *sin.* (2) God is right because the only answer to *sin* is the *cross!* Sinners are lost, without hope, and hell-bound. This offends us. Most of us cannot admit that we are lost enough to need salvation. Sinners do not wish to know, or to be reminded, of their guilt. Saying that we are sinners contradicts our proud, selfish, stubborn, and sinful hearts. Christ died for the ungodly, that is, for sinners (Romans 5:6–8). We all qualify!

The cross offends because sinners do not deserve, cannot earn, and cannot buy salvation. We see here the offense of grace! Man cannot save himself. However, what justice demanded, grace provided. Jesus paid it all. Sinful man is eternally helpless without Jesus! Man cannot imagine or explain the cross—he can only humbly believe in it. This offends us.

The cross offends because we cannot respond to God "our way." Jesus said, "I am the way, and the truth, and the life; no one comes to the Father but through Me" (John 14:6). His statement is rigid, narrow, exclusive, intolerant, and judgmental . . . but it is the truth. Such a declaration is offensive (see Acts 4:11, 12). Do we seek to please men or God? (John 12:42, 43; Acts 5:29). No sinner can be saved apart from Jesus. The time has come for us to put the cross where God put it. God Himself . . . gave Himself . . . to save us . . . from ourselves!

The cross . . .
there is no other way!

33

My Cross

Matthew 10:37–39; 16:24–26; Mark 8:34–37; Luke 9:23–25; 14:26, 27; Romans 6:1–11; Galatians 2:20, 21; 6:14; Philippians 1:21

"'And he who does not take his cross and follow after Me is not worthy of Me'" (Matthew 10:38).

Jesus had His cross, you have yours, and I have mine. It is easy to promote His; it is also easy to neglect yours and mine. If we do not accept ours, we cannot possess His. Unless we take up our crosses, His is in vain as far as our lives are concerned. I may not be able to change the world, but God can change me. No one can walk the path of righteousness for me. I must sacrifice the "Big Me" to receive the "Great He." The absolute good in me is Christ in me (Galatians 2:20, 21). On the cross Jesus died not only *instead* of us, but also *for* us.

We, too, die, suffer, and carry our crosses. He bore His; we also must bear ours. We have the gift of grace, but we also must have good works. Grace is not earned, but it demands our efforts. Salvation can never be "Come in, Savior, but stay out, Lord." Martin Luther King, Jr., well said, "The cross we bear precedes the crown we wear."[1] A cross around your neck can never substitute for a cross on your back.

There is no "cheap grace," and there are no cheap crosses. It is easy to be tolerant, but it is costly to practice true Christian love.

Let us keep going back to the text: "If anyone wishes to come after Me, he must deny himself, and take up his cross daily and follow Me" (Luke 9:23; see Matthew 16:24; Mark 8:34). What does it mean to take up my cross?

(1) *My cross is exclusive.* The command to take up a cross could be one of the greatest demands Jesus ever made. His condition is dogmatic, intolerant, mandatory, and eternally vital. Jesus said you are either "in" or "out." He gave no "ifs, ands, or buts." He said, "Whoever does not carry his own cross and come after Me cannot be My disciple" (Luke 14:27). He said, "So then, none of you can be My disciple who does not give up all his own possessions" (Luke 14:33). The cross calls for death. We must die to self, sin, and society. Crosses are costly. Basically, we have only three problems: "me, myself, and I." We must die to all three! Superficial views of the cross result in weak Christians. We cannot compromise the cross. The Christian life is not always easy and happy. Will we pay the price? Will we die to ourselves? Will we give up our rights to ourselves? Jesus is Lord. We must admit to being lost sinners and put our obedient faith in Him.

We know we need to believe in God. We also need to know that God believes in us. The power to live the Epistles is found in the story of the cross in the Gospels. We are pardoned—not paroled. We are not saved to live

---

[1]Martin Luther King, Jr., "Challenge to the Churches and Synagogues," *Challenge to Religion*, ed. Mathew Ahmann (Chicago: Henry Regnery Co., 1963), 168.

as convicts. We must never forget that God lives in us "to will and to work for His good pleasure" (Philippians 2:13). Christians must become vessels of honor (2 Timothy 2:20, 21). All of us must develop and maintain our own individual relationships with God. We cannot afford to live in doubt and visit our faith. We must live in faith and abandon our doubt.

(2) *My cross is daily.* "Ouch!" Daily? Christianity is a life—not a moment. Paul tersely said, ". . . I die daily" (1 Corinthians 15:31). Life is daily—and so is Christianity. We need daily bread (Matthew 6:11) and daily spiritual bread (Acts 17:11; Hebrews 3:13). The early church had daily additions (Acts 2:47; 16:5). A sinner, in order to receive salvation, must die to himself and take up his cross daily. These are two separate actions, not one. Do not confuse "self-denial" with "cross-bearing."

We need fresh forgiveness daily. Yesterday's forgiveness is not for today or tomorrow. We do not die once in conversion and stay dead. Daily death is a daily choice. We are to be Christians who are daily living a crucified life with Christ. As Christians, we . . .

. . . are facing only one direction.
. . . can never turn back.
. . . no longer have plans of our own.
. . . have minds through which Christ thinks.
. . . have hearts through which Christ loves.
. . . have voices through which Christ speaks.
. . . have bodies through which Christ serves.

Carry your cross until you find someone who needs it more than you do—then give it to him. (You never will.)

(3) *My cross is not one of my many burdens.* Too many think, "This burden must be my cross to bear." Jesus said

142

"cross," not "crosses." A cross is something we "take up," not something we "put up with." This kind of thinking reduces Christians to victims. Galatians 2:20, 21 is the most "self-filled" text in the Scriptures; it is also the most "self-surrendered" text in the Scriptures. Eight personal pronouns are used in the passage. "I" appears five times; "me" appears three. What is the great paradox? Self-crucifixion allows true life. One can neither kill nor hurt a dead man. Some of us are not totally dead. The man who has died to everything has the ability to give up anything. The Christian has to die before he can serve.

(4) *My cross is not misery or sadistic martyrdom.* My cross represents joy, not pessimistic "doom and gloom" (see John 15:11–14; Romans 14:17; 15:13; Hebrews 12:2; James 1:2; 1 John 1:4; 3 John 4). Sadly, we know about guilt, but we do not know about grace and gratitude. Do not teach self-sacrifice without joy. Do not reduce the gospel message to stoicism. Taking up the cross is positive, not negative; it is joyous, not miserable. It results in victorious living, not neurotic martyrdom. We are called to live in the "forgiveness of God."

(5) *My cross is accepting forgiveness and sharing salvation with others.* To take up my cross is to live forgiven, to forgive others, and to die to self so that I might teach and serve others (see 1 John 3:16–18). The cross is our call to forgive others. We cannot receive what we refuse to give. Until one accepts grace, he cannot learn mercy.

Each person "writes his own book on the cross" as he decides how he will respond to Jesus' sacrifice. I have written mine; now write yours!

The cross . . .
there is no other way!

143

34
Key Words and Phrases

We can easily review the totality of Christianity by thinking through the key words and phrases in which the story of Christ is expressed.

The Godhead: The name "God" might be thought of as a divine family name. The Godhead, or Trinity, is God the Father, God the Son (Jesus), and God the Spirit. God is one in essence and purpose, but three in personality and function (see 2 Corinthians 13:14). For example, at Jesus' baptism, Jesus was baptized, God the Father spoke from heaven, and the Holy Spirit descended upon Jesus in the form of a dove (Matthew 3:16, 17). See Acts 17:29; Romans 1:20; Colossians 2:9 in the KJV.

The holy Scriptures: The Bible is made up of sixty-six books (thirty-nine in the Old Testament and twenty-seven in the New Testament) that were given to us through the guidance and supervision of the Holy Spirit. They portray what God has done, what He is doing, and what He will do with those who want to be His children. The Old Testament is mainly divine history, while the New Testament is the last will and testament of Jesus for the Christian Age. See 2 Timothy 3:16, 17; 2 Peter 1:20, 21.

The incarnation: Jesus, the second member of the Godhead, actually became a man and lived among us. He is the Messiah that God had promised to send. He left heaven and became man without losing His identity as the Son of God. He was completely God and completely man. Only a God-Man could carry the burden of all the guilt of the world. See John 1:14; Philippians 2:5–8.

John the Baptist: God set this man apart to herald the coming of the Messiah. Through John's preaching, God prepared people for Jesus' coming. John personally identified Jesus as the Messiah. See Matthew 3:1–12; Mark 1:1–8; Luke 3:1–20; John 1:29.

The earthly ministry of Jesus: At age thirty, Jesus began an earthly ministry. For three-plus years He laid the foundation for His coming kingdom and for His death for our sins. During this time, He preached the gospel of the kingdom, healed the sick, and demonstrated what God is like. See Matthew 4:17; 11:4–6; Mark 1:14, 15.

Miracles: Supernatural acts were referred to as "miracles," "signs," and "wonders." They confirmed the divine power that Jesus possessed. He raised the dead, restored sight to the blind, cast out demons, and performed many other miracles. No one denied the miracles that were worked by Jesus, His apostles, or other inspired men of the first century. See John 20:30, 31; Hebrews 2:3, 4.

The fulfillment of prophecies (passion predictions): Jesus often foretold His coming trials and crucifixion. He gave details about what He was going to experience for the salvation of the world. See Matthew 16:21–23; 20:18, 19.

The Lord's Supper: As Jesus ate the Passover with His apostles on the night of His arrest, He instituted a supper of unleavened bread and fruit of the vine that He asked His followers to observe (Matthew 26:26–29; Mark 14:22–25; Luke 22:19, 20). The New Testament indicates that His followers ate of it regularly. This was done each Sunday, the first day of the week (Acts 20:7), when the early Christians came together for worship. In this service, they sang praises to God, prayed, participated in this Supper, considered His Word, and gathered a contribution for good works.

Gethsemane: Jesus frequently went to this garden to pray when He was in Jerusalem. Before His crucifixion, He went there to pray and finalize His plans to die for the sins of the world. His prayers in Gethsemane are the greatest prayers that have ever been prayed. See Matthew 26:36–46; Mark 14:32–42; Luke 22:39–46.

The Jewish trials: Rome had said to the Jews, "You may judge your own people, but you cannot put them to death unless they have violated your temple. If you seek capital punishment for anyone who has not violated your temple, you must get our agreement to carry it out." Therefore, the Jews took Jesus first to their Jewish leaders—Annas, Caiaphas, and the Sanhedrin—to put together a case against Jesus that they could present to the Roman authorities. They insisted that Rome agree with them and crucify Jesus. For Annas, see John 18:12, 13, 19–23; for Caiaphas, see Matthew 26:57; John 18:14, 24; for the Sanhedrin, see Matthew 26:59–68; 27:1, 2; Mark 14:53–65; 15:1; Luke 22:66—23:1.

The Roman trials: The Jews took Jesus to Pilate, who would be the representative of Rome. Pilate did not agree with their case, but he did not want a riot. He was pushed into a corner and finally gave in to their request. For the first trial before Pilate, see Luke 23:1–7; for Herod, see Luke 23:8–11; for the second trial before Pilate, see Luke 23:11–25.

The crucifixion: This was a cruel way of executing a criminal by nailing him to a cross, or tree, until he died (Galatians 3:13). Suffering was prolonged in some cases for days. A Roman citizen could not be scourged or crucified. The Jews normally used stoning as their means of executing someone; but in Jesus' case, they demanded crucifixion. See Matthew 27:33–54; Mark 15:20–39; Luke 23:32–47; John 19:17–30.

The resurrection: After being in the grave for parts of three days (Friday, Saturday, and Sunday), Jesus arose from the dead, demonstrating that He had power over death. His miraculous resurrection indicated that He was indeed the second member of the Godhead. See Matthew 28; Mark 16; Luke 24; John 20; 21.

The ascension: Forty days after Jesus' resurrection, He ascended to heaven. The apostles were present when He ascended through the clouds back to the Father's side. The Scriptures declare that He will return at the end of time in a similar way (Matthew 26:64). See Luke 24:51; Acts 1:9–11.

The Day of Pentecost: The Day of Pentecost was ten days after Jesus' ascension. This was one of the three main feasts of the Jews. On this day, the Holy Spirit was poured out upon the apostles as a sign of the coming of the new covenant and to equip them to speak and write God's message faithfully and accurately. When the gospel was preached, three thousand people repented and were baptized for the forgiveness of their sins. On this day the church that Jesus promised came into existence. See Acts 2.

Faith: This is the attitude of accepting Jesus as God's Son, believing what God has said, and acting upon His words with trust and love. See Romans 10:17; Hebrews 11:1.

Repentance: The attitude of stopping behavior that we know to be evil or sinful and turning in obedience to the Word of God is repentance. The resolve of the penitent heart is to follow with joy and commitment what God teaches us to do in the Christian Age. See Acts 17:30; 1 Thessalonians 1:9, 10.

Confession: This is both a verbal declaration that we believe that Jesus Christ is the Son of God and a life-demonstration of His deity. See Matthew 10:32; Romans 10:10; 1 John 4:15.

Baptism: One is baptized when he or she is immersed in water for the forgiveness of sins. Baptism is an act of faith and a re-enacting of the death, burial, and resurrection of Christ. It is the moment when Jesus adds the one who is immersed to His church. See Matthew 28:19, 20; Acts 2:38, 41, 47; Romans 6:3, 4.

The church: Also called the "body" or the "kingdom" of Christ, the church is Christ's spiritual body that contains the saved. His body worships God and does His work in the world. Jesus did His work in an earthly body when He was here, but now He does His work through His spiritual body, the church. See Ephesians 1:22, 23; 3:21.

Sanctification: The Christian is sanctified, or set apart by the Lord, at his baptism. He continues to grow in this sanctification throughout his life on earth. He becomes more like God in holiness and purity as he studies God's Word, worships, prays, gives, forgives, and serves those who need his help. See 1 Corinthians 1:1, 2; Acts 20:32; Hebrews 2:11; 10:14.

"How Should We Respond To Jesus' Death?"

by Ian Terry

In reading this book, perhaps our hearts have been touched by the inestimable love that God and Jesus have for all humanity. We have been impressed by the awfulness of the sin of mankind that would require such a costly sacrifice. Surely, we desire to have a harmonious relationship with God, who loves us so much and wants to lavish His blessings upon us for all eternity.

How, then, can we obtain the salvation and forgiveness that Jesus made available through the cross? How can we receive the eternal life that Jesus agonized to provide?

Let us consider the following questions. God will give us the answers through His Word as we read the related Scriptures. What will *your* response be at the close of the study?

1. Why do people need the forgiveness that Jesus died to provide? (Romans 3:9–18, 23) _____
   Does this include you? _____

2. What must we do first to receive the forgiveness and eternal life that Jesus came to give? (John 3:16, 17; 8:24)
   _____

   Who must we believe that Jesus is? (Matthew 1:18–25)
   _____

   Why is it so important to believe in Jesus? (John 14:6; Acts 4:12) _____
   What must we believe that Jesus did to make it possible for us to be forgiven? (Matthew 20:28; Romans 5:8, 9)
   _____

   Do you believe in Jesus? _____

3. What is the next element in our response to Jesus? (Acts 17:30; 26:20) _____
What is repentance, and why is it essential? (Acts 3:19; Luke 13:3) _____
What considerations motivate us to repent? (Romans 2:4; 2 Thessalonians 1:7–9; 1 Peter 1:18, 19) _____
Are you going to turn your back on the sin that crucified Jesus and follow Him? _____

4. What is the third step in accepting Jesus' forgiveness? (Romans 10:9, 10) _____
Why is it so important to acknowledge Jesus and give our allegiance to Him? (Matthew 10:32, 33; 1 Timothy 6:12, 13) _____
Are you ready to confess your faith in Christ? _____

5. What is the final act of faith and obedience, at which point our sins are forgiven and we are saved? (Mark 16:16; Acts 2:38) _____
How does the Bible express the purpose of baptism? (Acts 22:16) _____
Is Bible baptism sprinkling, pouring, or immersion? (Acts 8:35–39; Romans 6:3, 4) _____
How does baptism relate to Jesus' death, burial, and resurrection? (Romans 6:3–11) _____

YOUR RESPONSE

Now that God, through His Word, has shown you how to respond to Jesus in receiving salvation and forgiveness, are you ready to turn your back on sin and follow Him?

Are you ready to acknowledge Him as Lord and be buried and raised with Him through baptism, in the likeness of His saving act, for the forgiveness of your sins?

If you are ready to take this step of faith, contact the nearest church of Christ, and someone will assist you. If you are not sure where the church is located, go to **www.churchzip.com** and type your location or e-mail **staff@alltheworld2015.org**.

A Final Note

The Agony & Glory of the Cross has been provided as a gift from the churches of Christ. The subject matter of the book was chosen because it represents the heart of the message that we strive to preach and teach. We believe that it is the heart of the teaching of the New Testament. The churches of Christ are committed to following the New Testament as their only creed for salvation and worship and as their standard for daily living. Although we are not perfect, we desire above all else to be CHRIST-ians, that is, followers of Christ.

If we can help you in any way, please call on the church of Christ nearest to you. Here is a website that may help you to find the location where it is meeting: **www.churchzip.com**. We especially would be delighted to get to know you and encourage you, if we can, in your walk with Christ.

If you would like help with further study of the Bible, we will be happy to provide a free copy of the book *Into the Abundant Life*, which discusses more thoroughly how to become a Christian. Just ask the person who gave you this book on the cross to get one for you, and he or she will be glad to do it. If that person is unavailable to you, please go to the website **www.alltheworld2015.org** and ask for the book; it will promptly be mailed to you or brought to you by a member of the church.

We are so happy that you have read this book. Think deeply about its message. Let us stand together at the foot of the cross. As another has said, "With Jesus we cannot lose, and without Him, we cannot win."

Contact Information

To learn more about the Bible, visit
www.biblecourses.com
www.wbschool.org
www.searchtv.org

If you want help in applying
the message of the cross to your life,
ask the person who gave you this book
for a copy of *Into the Abundant Life*
or contact one of the following:

Truth for Today
P.O. Box 2044
Searcy, Arkansas 72145-2044
phone: 501-268-7588
e-mail: staff@alltheworld2015.org

The nearest church of Christ
(located through www.churchzip.com)